HIDDEN HISTORY *of the* GRAND STRAND

HIDDEN HISTORY *of the* GRAND STRAND

Rick Simmons

THE History PRESS

Published by The History Press
Charleston, SC 29403
www.historypress.net

Cover image by Mike Burton

First published 2010

Manufactured in the United States

ISBN 978.1.59629.966.5

Simmons, Rick.
Hidden history of the Grand Strand / Rick Simmons.
p. cm.
Includes bibliographical references.
ISBN 978-1-59629-966-5
1. Myrtle Beach Region (S.C.)--History. 2. Myrtle Beach Region (S.C.)--History, Local. 3. Historic buildings--South Carolina--Myrtle Beach Region. 4. Historic sites--South Carolina--Myrtle Beach Region. 5. Georgetown County (S.C.)--History, Local. I. Title.
F279.M93S56 2010
975.7'89--dc22
2010017386

Contents

Preface

I must admit that I'm surprised and delighted to find that, just one year after writing a very similar acknowledgements page for my book *Defending South Carolina's Coast: The Civil War from Georgetown to Little River*, I'm once again doing the same thing for yet another book from The History Press. Like my first book, this was not a volume that just appeared overnight, despite what one might think because of the short time between the two publications. Just as my last book originated in the early 1990s with a series of historical articles in South Carolina–based magazines, this book also drew on a few pieces I had written nearly twenty years ago. The chapters herein dealing with Old Gunn Church, the U-boat enigma and the Hot and Hot Fish Club are, at least in part, based on articles I published some time ago, although the extensive research I did on North Island, the Ocean Forest and the disappearing landmarks is all new (and concerning topics I never got to write about the first time around). It's likely that I would have written about these things at some point had I remained living at the beach, but when we left the coast so that I could pursue a PhD, my nonacademic writing career went on a twenty-year hiatus. I earned my master's degree and PhD and moved to Louisiana, where I became, and am currently, a professor at Louisiana Tech University.

As my wife and I raised our children, and as I spent my time publishing the things required for tenure and promotion, there was little time to return to those topics I had researched and thought about in the early 1990s. We would vacation at our family home on Pawleys Island every summer, sometimes spending as much as a month there, and during those trips I would occasionally think about and visit the places of interest covered in this book. However, living one thousand miles away and with little time for writing as a hobby, thinking about it is about as far as it went.

Once I had tenure, and then after being promoted to full professor, I felt that it was time to revisit the topics I had addressed so many years before. My first order of business was to finish my book about the Civil War, *Defending South Carolina's Coast*, and after being fortunate enough to place it with the exceptional History Press, I decided to put together a book based on some other topics I had investigated so long ago. Within a year, I was ready with what was to become this book, and Laura All, the great commissioning editor at The History Press, informed me that they would like to pick up the option on this book as well.

So here I sit, elated that *Hidden History of the Grand Strand* will complete the cycle of those individually themed topics about which I also wanted to write a book but never had time to address. I expect I'll have to move in another direction next time.

A few people deserve mention here for a variety of reasons. Once again, Scott Lawrence unselfishly and on a number of occasions took my family out boating in Winyah Bay and Murrells Inlet to visit the islands. I also thank him for running out to snap a few updated pictures of the *Harvest Moon* and Battery White, for letting me use them in this book and for taking us out in his boat to Drunken Jack Island in the cold of winter of December 2009 so that I could examine what might have been, and what I think proved to be, the remains of Fort Ward. Of course my wife Sue, daughter Courtenay and son Cord have always been supportive, but the problem is that with each book I publish about the area, my wife becomes further convinced that it's another sign that we need to move back home! My father and sister have always been supportive, and so I owe them thanks as well. Between Julie and Dad, I'm able to take my family back to South Carolina, stay weeks at a time and visit and research these places I like to write about.

Robin Salmon, vice-president for collections and curator of sculpture at Brookgreen Gardens, helped me with information yet again, and I thank her for all she has done for both books now. I'd like to thank Jack Shaum of the Steamship Historical Society of America, who may be world's greatest expert on the *City of Richmond* and was gracious enough to lend me his one-of-a-kind pictures of that ship. Jamie Dozier, project leader at the Tom Yawkey Wildlife Center, was also very helpful, and I appreciate his information about North Island. Jill Santopietro, director of the Georgetown County Museum, gave me information as well. Jennifer Ledet helped me with some picture problems I had. I appreciate the Pawleys Island Civic Association for letting me use the fantastic photographs in its collection. Julie Warren, with the Georgetown County Digital Library, went above and beyond the call of duty, getting permission for me to use photographs again and again, and I'm not sure anyone could have helped me more, or have been more gracious, than Julie. I'd also like to thank my old friend, college roommate and fraternity brother, Steve Bond. Sometimes you just need someone outside your family to really believe in what you're doing, and I couldn't have had a more ardent supporter than I had in him on this and my previous book—thanks Bondo (and Margaret, too). Finally, I thank those of you who will buy this book. Publishers print them because of you, and you have my sincerest thanks.

Chapter 1

Historic North Island

North Island is arguably the most colorful and historically important area along the Grand Strand. It may well have been the site of the first recorded shipwreck in North America, it probably would have been the site of the first Spanish settlement in America, it was one of the first vacation resorts in America and it still is the location of the oldest existing lighthouse in South Carolina (and one of the oldest lighthouses in the United States). Based on its historical importance, one could easily write an entire book about North Island, yet today the island sits completely uninhabited, home to a few crumbling and unoccupied buildings and a now-automated lighthouse. How did this important island go from being home to a village—replete with a church, a school, a proposed base for British troops, Confederate and Union forts and a flourishing resort—to an abandoned island today? The answers are as intriguing as the questions.

The island's first brush with fame was short-lived, and had it not been for an untimely shipwreck at North Island, the history of North America may have taken a very different course indeed. Lucas Vazquez de Ayllon's flagship, the *Capitana*, was one of a fleet of a half-dozen Spanish ships headed for the vicinity of what is now Georgetown in order to establish a settlement in the New World. In 1526, De Ayllon's flagship grounded, probably near the entrance to Winyah Bay at North Island. The ship was laden with a cargo of cattle, three thousand barrels of olive oil and enough food and supplies to establish a colony in the New World that would have predated the Spanish colony at St. Augustine, Florida. With the expedition's supplies lost (though the crew fortunately survived), the Spaniards went south instead of settling

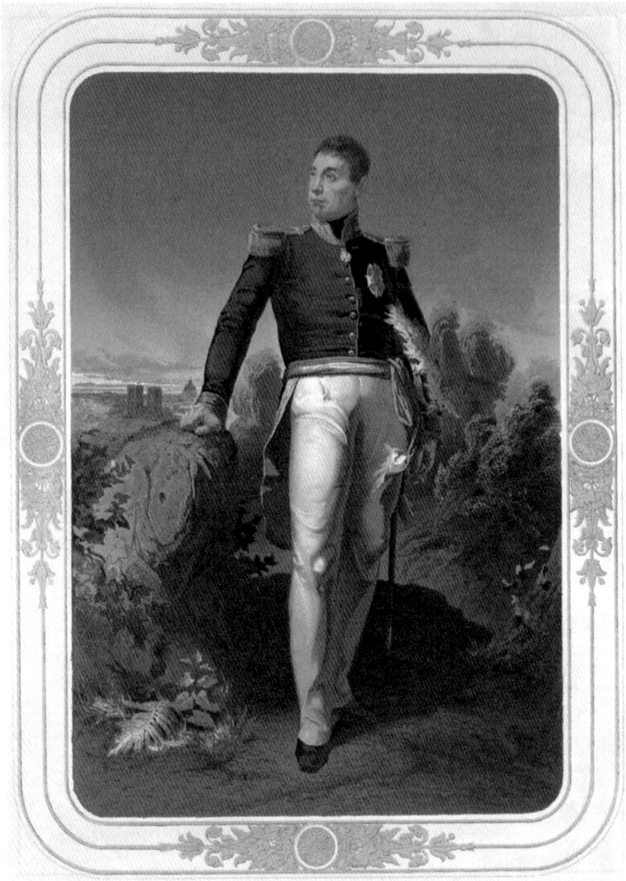

On a dark night in 1777, the Marquis de Lafayette landed on North Island and visited the home of Benjamin Huger. Today, a marker on Highway 17 outside of Georgetown commemorates that event. *Courtesy Library of Congress.*

in this area. Had the Spanish colony been established near Georgetown, that area would have been the first settled in the state, and the history of this state would have been significantly different.

Archaeologists continue to search for the ship even today, but Christopher Amer of the South Carolina Institute of Archaeology and Anthropology has noted that the search is difficult because the ship could even be "under…North Island somewhere." In 1526, North Island was shorter on the southern end and would have been quite different; consequently, the mystery of the location of what was the area's most important shipwreck, and North Island's first brush with recorded history, may never be known.

Even though the Spanish never established a permanent settlement on the island, the British (and soon-to-be Americans) did. By the late eighteenth century, area residents—especially those wealthy enough to have both a home on the mainland and a vacation home—appreciated the salubrious effects of the cool ocean breezes; a number of wealthy individuals established residence on the island, especially for the summer months. It was during one such summer sojourn that perhaps the most important historical event to take place on North Island occurred. On June 13, 1777, Major Benjamin Huger of the South Carolina militia was residing at his summer home on the island when he was alerted by the sounds of his dogs barking late one night. Fearing that British troops may have landed on the island, Huger was preparing to defend his home when, instead, a knock at the door revealed two travelers who had arrived by ship. The men told Huger that they were from Bordeaux, France, and that after a fifty-four-day sea voyage they had landed on North Island hoping to find a pilot to navigate their ship through local waters.

Huger invited the men—the soon-to-be-famous Marquis de Lafayette and Baron de Kalb—to stay with him, and for two days Huger entertained them in his home. Huger's goodwill and patriotic fervor no doubt increased their respect for the American spirit once they left to join George Washington and fight for the cause of American independence. As a result, Lafayette's landing has long been seen as a signature event in the island's history; a notice in the *Winyah Observer* of August 21, 1850, indicates that during the nineteenth century the island was referred to as both North and "Lafayette Island," and even today a historical marker on Highway 17 commemorates Lafayette's landing.

Huger's trepidation about who alerted him that late night was not without reason. Because North Island guarded the entrance to Winyah Bay, which was a somewhat significant anchorage, opposing military forces would be interested in the island over the next eighty years and through three wars. The first of many mentions of the island as a strategic location occurred on July 11, 1780, when Major James Wemyss wrote to Lord Cornwallis and asked if he could station his British troops, then in Georgetown, in the more hospitable climate of North Island. Cornwallis, however, was worried about American troops under the command of General Horatio Gates, and he refused Wemyss's request and instead ordered the British troops to Camden.

After the Revolutionary War ended in 1783, the fledgling United States had to cope with a number of issues as it struggled to build a new nation, and for a country so dependent on shipping, lighthouses were essential for coastal safety. To that end, the construction of the first lighthouse on North Island was especially significant. Built on a tract of land donated by the planter and Patriot Paul Trapier in 1789, the lighthouse was begun in 1799 with a federal appropriation of $5,000 and was completed on February 14, 1801. This seventy-two-foot-tall octagonal structure was built of cypress and burned whale oil to light its lamp. This first incarnation of the Georgetown lighthouse was destroyed by a hurricane in 1806, and in 1807 Congress allotted $20,000 for a new lighthouse to be built out of stone to withstand the high winds that frequently swept the island during storms. By 1811, the sturdier lighthouse was functional and would be one of only four between Delaware and Florida. This lighthouse burned whale oil as well and required a full-time lighthouse keeper.

At about this same time, an extremely ambitious engineering project was formulated for North Island—a great canal that would be cut across the island to provide more direct access to Winyah Bay and the port of Georgetown. The entrance to Winyah Bay between North and South Islands was treacherous and shallow, so much so that by the twentieth century costly rock jetties would have to be built to open up the passage to large ships. John Drayton's 1802 work, *A View of South Carolina, as Respects Her Natural and Civil Concerns*, contains one of the earliest mentions of the plan for the "highly advantageous canal," and Drayton notes that such a canal would mean that the approach to Georgetown "will be attended with greater safety, and its commerce be much increased by admitting vessels of heavier burden than those which can penetrate the channel between North and South Islands."

The plan was to cut a canal from a point north of the lighthouse and running east to west from the ocean on the other side of North Island, where the water was twenty-four feet deep, to Winyah Bay, where the water was eighteen feet deep, which would enable ships to avoid the treacherous sandbars at the mouth of the bay. The federal government approved $20,000 to build this canal under the direction of State Engineer (and lieutenant colonel) Christian Senf; the superintendents of the project, Savage Smith, Joseph Alston, Charles Brown, Robert Grant and Samuel Taylor, oversaw the construction of the canal.

Though not all area residents were convinced that the canal was a good idea—Peter Horry worried that the change in water conditions would be detrimental to the rice harvest—work began as the digging commenced from the Winyah Bay side of North Island. Then, just as the canal was about to break through to the ocean, a hurricane hit the coast and filled in at least one-third of the canal from the ocean side of the island. Faced with the obvious conclusion—that such occurrences would beset the canal again and again given the area's weather—the ambitious project proved impractical and was never finished. Even today, more than two hundred years later, satellite images of the island clearly show at least a half-mile of the remaining canal that was completed before being abandoned.

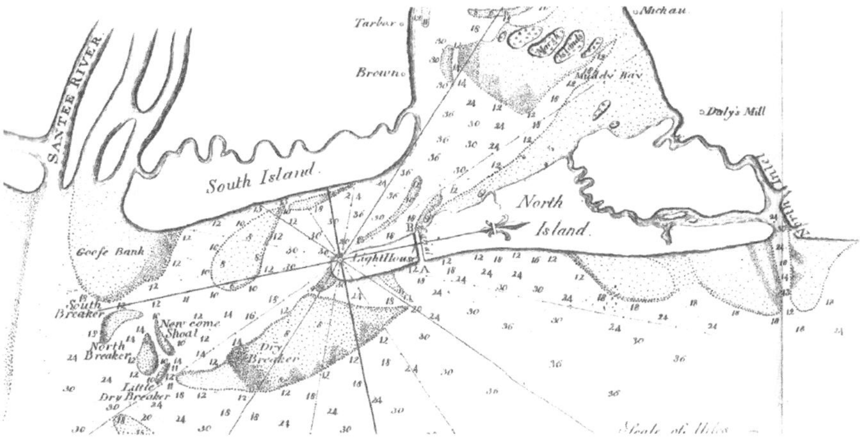

One of the most remarkable engineering projects in the young United States began at North Island about 1805. As this map from 1802 shows, the canal would be cut across the island so that ships could avoid the dangerous sandbars at the entrance to Winyah Bay and, instead, enter straight into the bay from the ocean.

During the War of 1812, American militia were posted on North Island, and although British warships were responsible for several wrecks, including the prize brig *Tartar*, which was chased ashore at North Island in April 1813, no military operations of note took place on the island. The hurricane of 1813, which wrecked as many as five ships on the island, did far more damage to shipping in the area than the British. Hurricanes, in fact, would always be the bane of any individuals who wanted to inhabit the island, and the storms would play a significant role in the construction and reconstruction of the dwellings on the island, as they had with the proposed canal.

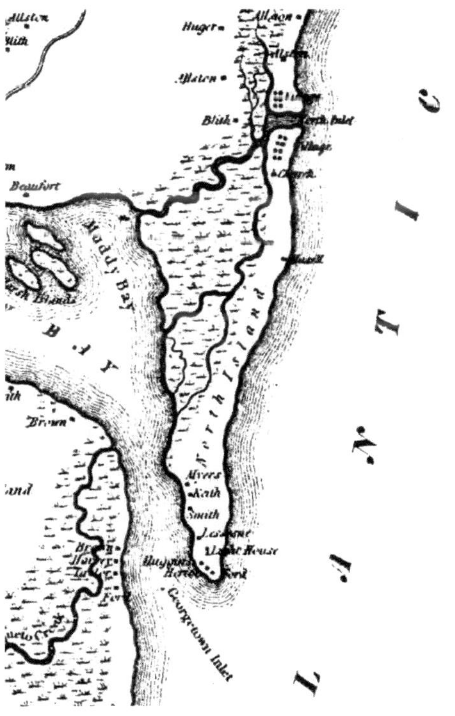

This *Mills Atlas Map of 1825* shows a sizeable village, as well as a church, near North Inlet. Repeated hurricanes would eventually destroy all habitations on the island.

The greatest development North Island would ever see took place in the early nineteenth century. By 1820, North Island had become a relaxation retreat and was, in fact, the area's first resort—more than a century before Myrtle Beach was even conceived. Increasingly, wealthy rice planters were building vacation homes on the island, and other, more permanent habitations were being built as well. A summer community known as La Grange had existed on the island during the 1700s, and in the 1800s a village of more than one hundred houses called Lafayette Village was built at North Inlet, replete with a church. The circa 1820 drawings for the *Mill's Atlas*, published in 1825, show the village and church, as well as a number of plantation homes around the circumference of the island. But the idyllic conditions on the island would not last long.

A hurricane in 1820 caused the tide to rise four feet above normal, resulting in substantial damage to structures on the island, and the hurricane of September 27 and 28, 1822, destroyed many of the homes and killed a number of residents. According to records of the period, the tides rose so high that very little of the island was above water, and there were as many as 125 drownings on North Island alone—perhaps as many as 300 people died. During that hurricane, witnesses noticed whole houses floating out to sea, and one account from the period notes a family clinging to the branches of a tree as, one by one, they dropped into the swirling waters below them; all but two of them drowned.

Despite the almost total devastation, some of the habitations were rebuilt once again, and by 1825 there was also school on the island. Robert Mills wrote in 1826 that as many as six or seven hundred people were on the island during the summer. Another major hurricane in September 1834 was so powerful that it wrecked at least five ships in the area, and hurricanes in 1846 and 1854 were also devastating. But with each passing storm, there was less rebuilding, and the buffeting of the island by a succession of storms made the area perhaps far less appealing than it had once been. To further complicate matters when living or rebuilding on the island, the island was practically inaccessible other than by boat and an occasional bridge that had to rebuilt after every major storm, and thus supplying the island was somewhat of a chore in the best of times. Therefore, after a long string of early nineteenth-century storms that devastated homes, flooded the island repeatedly and caused considerable loss of life, by the late nineteenth century the idea of building a permanent community on the island, living there for any length of time and expecting any structures to remain inhabitable for long had essentially been abandoned.

No matter what the island's weaknesses were as a resort area, there was no disputing its importance as a strategic position in times of war, and the Civil War saw the island serve as home to troops from both sides, as well as be the location of a number of naval encounters and skirmishes. When the Ordinance of Secession was signed in Charleston on December 20, 1860, area militia began preparing for the beginning of hostilities that they knew were sure to come, and camps of instruction and fortifications were established from Georgetown to Little River. The Confederates established Camp Norman on North Island near the lighthouse, and when earthen fortifications were planned for rivers and bays along the coast, it was clear that the Georgetown lighthouse was important strategically because it provided a lookout post that was undoubtedly the highest accessible point on the coast. As a result, as early as February 1861, mention of a redoubt named Fort Alston appears as being located on North Island, and at the beginning of the war it appears that Company D and Company B of what would become the Tenth South Carolina Regiment were stationed there in nearby Camp Norman.

A letter dated February 22, 1861, from John R. Beaty of the Tenth South Carolina Regiment, mentions that "the cannon at Fort Alston are firing and the balls pass down the Bay…they are practicing range to be ready…it has an ugly sound but I suppose I can get used to it." As for conditions on North Island, Beaty wrote that "it is a bleak barren row of sandhills exposed to the ocean on one side and Winyah Bay on the other…covered with a thick grove of pine and palmetto, very hilly and broken and a most capital place for riflemen to skirmish." In 1861, there was also for a time a small fort on the north end of the island (at various times companies A, E, H and K of the Tenth Regiment were stationed there), though it appears that this fort did not mount any artillery and was only periodically armed with the mobile fieldpieces of the Waccamaw Light Artillery. In April 1861, Major William Capers White notes having posted Captain Thomas West Daggett, two officers and twenty-six men of the Waccamaw Light Artillery on coast watch on North Island, and thus the fort on the north end of the island may have been simply a base with some earthworks but not a major fortification.

There was clearly a need for forts on the island, not only to protect the bay, but also to deal with the wrecked ships—blockade runners *and* warships—that were constantly beached on the island. On November 2, 1861, the Union steamer *Osceola* foundered off Georgetown, and two boats of captive crewmen were detained on North Island. On December 24, 1861, the USS *Gem of the Sea* attacked a beached runner, *Prince of Wales*, there. The next day, a Union transport ship loaded with troops passed so close to North Island that the soldiers on board could clearly be seen by the Confederates on the island, and so despite the fact that the North Island fort was little more than a base for Confederate troops as opposed to a practical tactical bastion, it was important that the Confederates maintained a presence there.

Eventually, though, when General John Pemberton took command of the military district that included Georgetown and North Island on March 14, 1862, he made the unpopular and controversial decision to withdraw all Confederate troops from and abandon the forts in the area, including Fort Alston. Not long afterward, in May 1862, the Federals realized that the island forts were undefended, and the USS *Albatross* and the steamer USS *Norwich* entered Winyah Bay. They noted that when they passed North Island, the redoubt and lighthouse were deserted, as had been similar forts on South and Cat Islands. Union troops landed, and North Island was then officially in Federal hands and would remain so for the duration of the war.

The Federals would make better use of the island than had the Confederates, however. After sailing into Georgetown on May 22, the *Albatross* and the *Norwich* proceeded up the Waccamaw River and raided a mill, carrying off eighty slaves in the process. The ships returned to North Island and disembarked the slaves, the first members of a "contraband" colony that was to grow quickly. Soon, hundreds of slaves began flocking to North Island, and before long more than seven hundred contrabands appear to have been under Federal protection there.

The Federals were never entirely happy with this situation, as it took a considerable troop presence to protect the former slaves and utilized precious supplies to feed them—much to their chagrin. There was also great concern that the Confederates would attempt to raid the island to kill the contrabands, and Prentiss had his boats constantly shelling the woods on North Island to disperse any Confederates who might try to approach the new Federal camps. On May 25, he reported that "there is not now a solitary Rebel on North… Island," and that as an added protection he had "destroyed the last remaining bridge which connects with the mainland, and there is no longer danger from incursion of cavalry, the only arm that is efficient or dares venture down here."

Despite his bravado, the situation on North Island remained an uneasy one at best. In 1862, Commander I.B. Baxter of the *Gem of the Sea* noted that there were about "500 troops at Georgetown, consisting of cavalry, infantry, and artillery, who intend crossing over in boats from Georgetown to [Pawleys] Island and from thence to the north end of North Island, with the intention of destroying the contrabands." Although the intended raid never amounted to more than a rumor, by that time the colony numbered more than 1,000 contrabands, and later more than 1,700 escaped slaves flocked to the Federal lines. By March 1863, Union admiral Samuel DuPont ordered the contraband colony removed by the USS *Sebago* and sent to Port Royal, and that eliminated the threat of a Confederate massacre once and for all.

The last major event of note involving North Island during the Civil War took place on June 2, 1864, when the USS *Wamsutta* chased the side-wheel steamer *Rose* to ground on North Island. A Union sentry in the North Island lighthouse spotted the ship lying close offshore near North Inlet at about 9:00 that morning, and the *Wamsutta* went in pursuit. The *Rose* ran ashore near the wreck of another steamer, and men from the *Wamsutta* boarded it. A force of about seventy-five Confederate cavalrymen came from the direction of the north end of the island. The Union sailors attempted to attach a rope from the *Rose* to the *Wamsutta* and tow it off, but the runner was firmly mired in the sand and would not budge. By this time, the *Wamsutta*'s captain noted that "the cavalry had advanced to the edge of the woods, and commenced firing at our men on board the steamer, who returned their fire, and I also shelled the woods, which kept them back." Eventually, rather than have any valuable supplies fall into Confederate hands, the Federals burned the *Rose*. Nevertheless, as late as June 9, Confederates were reported attempting to salvage machinery from the wreck.

Despite the fact that the North Island redoubt was of no real importance as a fort, the lighthouse and the island's location at the mouth of Winyah Bay ensured that the fort would always be of interest to both sides, and North Island was the Federals' major land base of operations along the Strand until Georgetown surrendered in 1865. As the Confederate forces in Georgetown faced further reductions in troops, little thought was given to trying to regain a foothold on North Island. Though it is not recorded or known who did it, either the Federals or the Confederates burned the lighthouse during the war, so that it had to be at least partially rebuilt after the war in 1867. That provided the basis of the structure that exists today, which is eighty-seven feet tall with a base diameter of twenty feet and a wall thickness of six inches.

For roughly the next fifty years, there was not much of an attempt to maintain anything more than a lighthouse keeper's residence on the island, a decision made simple due to further devastating hurricanes in 1881, 1885, 1893, 1903, 1906, 1910 and 1911. However, even with the threat of storms, it was hard to ignore the great island at the mouth of the bay sitting practically deserted and being underutilized in its potential as the resort for which it had long been recognized.

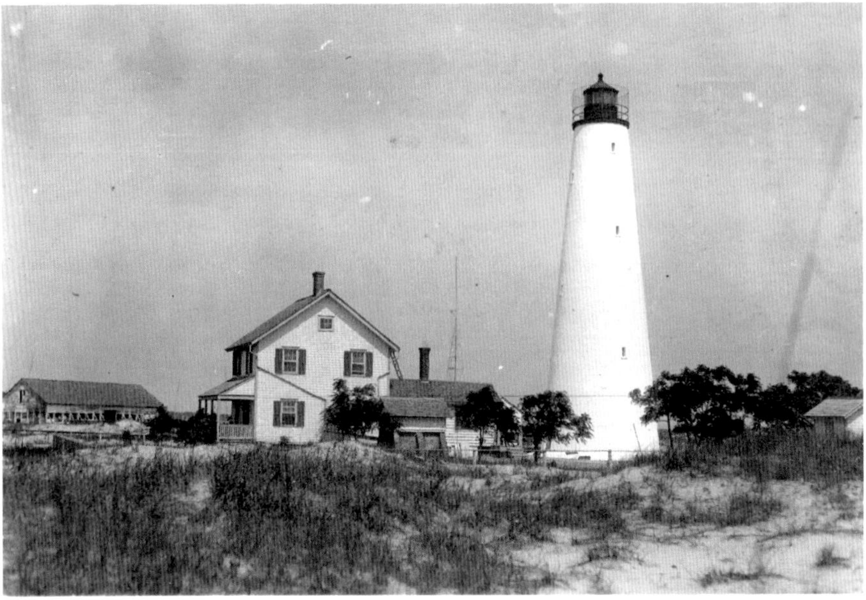

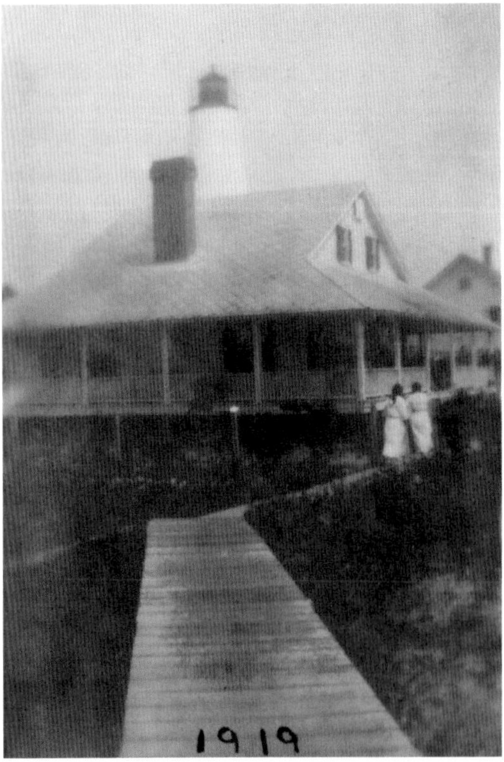

This page: As these pictures illustrate, since the first lighthouse was built in 1801, the area and buildings surrounding the light have gone through many changes. *Pictures courtesy Pawleys Island Civic Association and the Georgetown County Digital Library.*

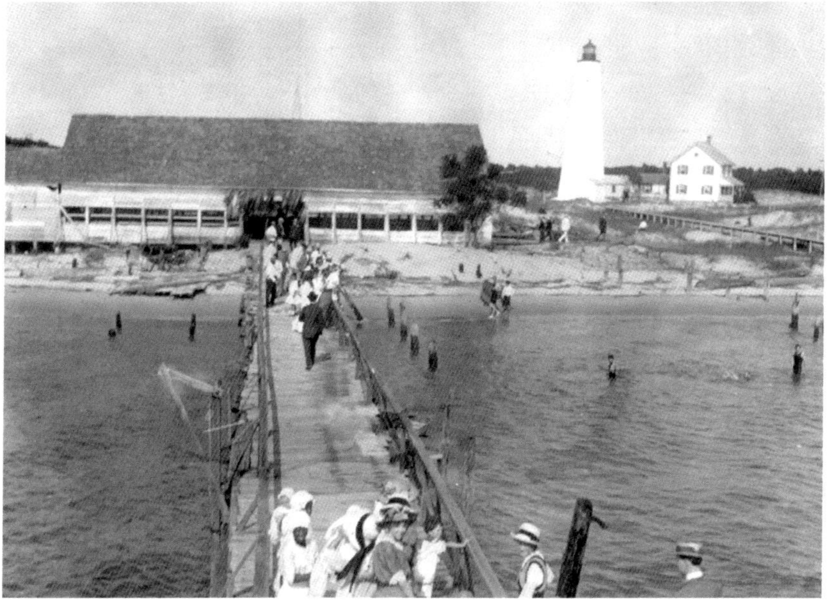

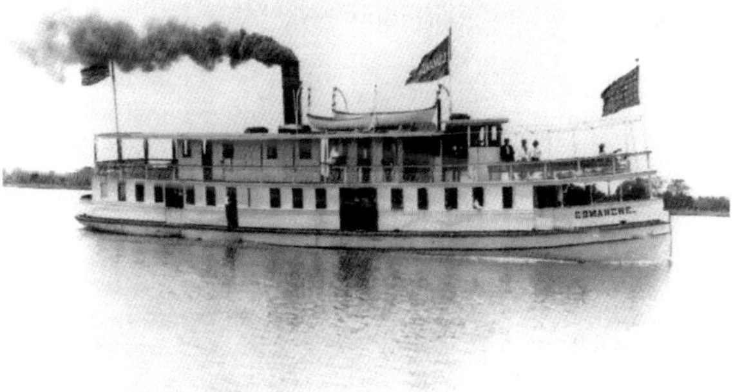

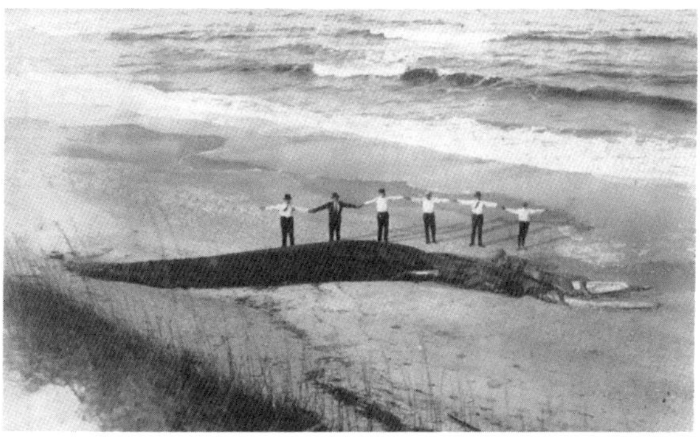

This page: As these photos show, by the early twentieth century North Island had once again been developed as a resort area for weekend getaways. The pavilion drew large crowds, and every Sunday afternoon boatloads of people traveled to the island in the steamer *Comanche*. Lucky visitors might even find the carcass of a whale, as these men did in 1921. *Courtesy Pawleys Island Civic Association and the Georgetown County Digital Library.*

While it was obvious that the island was impractical as the setting for a large, permanent settlement, using the island as a site of leisure activities seemed safe enough. A second pier and a pavilion were built on North Island near the lighthouse, and in the 1920s, B.A. Munnerlyn and Company offered weekly Sunday afternoon excursions to the island on the steamer *Comanche*. Pictures from the period show that it was apparently a popular weekend destination, but at some point the pier and pavilion disappeared; in fact, there is little evidence today that they ever existed. This is also true of a number of other structures that appear in pictures taken over the last 150 years. A lighthouse keeper's house, an assistant keeper's house, navy barracks, stables, a boathouse and many other structures appear in various photographs taken since the 1880s, yet today these structures have all vanished.

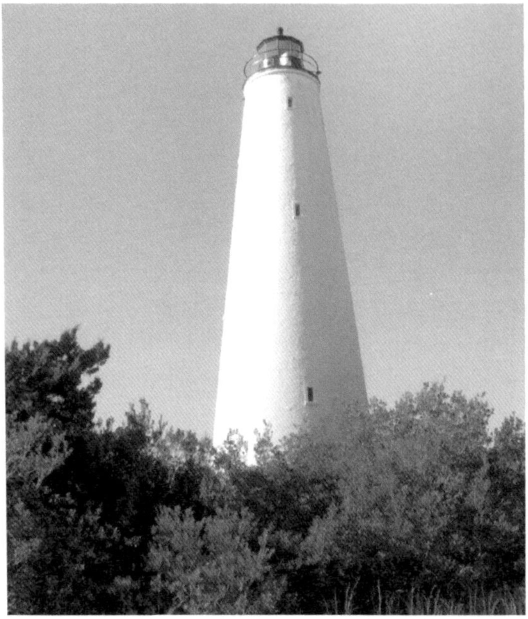

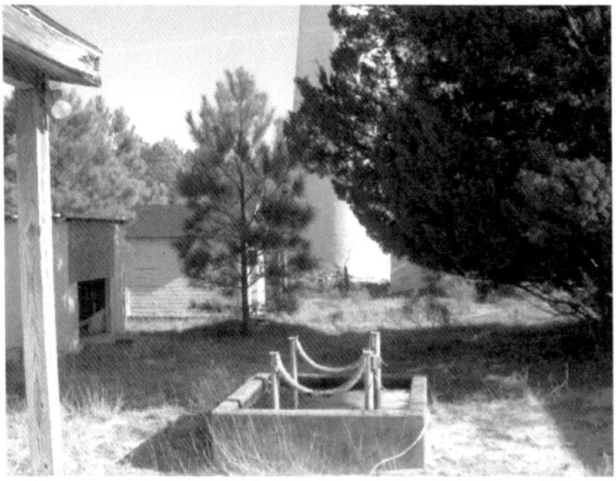

This page: Today, the abandoned Coast Guard station at North Island is a veritable ghost town of deserted beaches and empty buildings. No humans live on the island. *Photographs by the author.*

First the navy and then the Coast Guard maintained a presence on the island, and in the 1980s, the Coast Guard finally abandoned its post there by automating the lighthouse in 1986. About two years later, the Department of Juvenile Justice established a marine rehabilitation program for juvenile offenders on the island, but the program was eventually discontinued. Even those last-built facilities near the lighthouse have rapidly deteriorated, and the buildings sit isolated and abandoned; in all likelihood, wind and tide will cause them to disappear soon as well.

Today, North Island is a part of the Tom Yawkey Wildlife Preserve. The Yawkey Preserve encompasses roughly thirty-one square miles of protected island land, and while this has kept the land from being developed, it also means that it is largely off-limits to the public. Nevertheless, it staggers the mind to see such a massive, pristine tract of undeveloped coastal property. The island is lush and overgrown with vegetation, and in some places the beach has eroded to the point that it edges the forestation. Everywhere there are minute remnants of man's former presence there, but the island is devoid of human life. As a result, it is a peaceful place that offers a marked contrast to the bustle of the rest of the Grand Strand.

A NORTH ISLAND MYSTERY

Someone once noted that the Grand Strand must have more ghosts per square mile than any place in America. And while this is certainly not a book of ghost stories, there are a couple of ghostly tales about the island, and one has a source so reputable that it bears repeating here. One of the oldest ghost stories concerning the island is the ubiquitous-type haunting tale from the 1800s about a lighthouse keeper and his daughter, Annie. After a trip to the mainland, their boat was swamped in a storm, and so the lighthouse keeper tied his daughter to his back and started to swim. After making it ashore, he collapsed and later awakened to find his drowned daughter still tied to his back. In the late nineteenth and early twentieth centuries, the local legend was that Annie would appear to sailors in the area before a storm and stand on the decks of their ships, warning them to "go back, go back."

The first assistant lighthouse keeper's house on the island (now gone, of course) was claimed to be uninhabitable because it was also haunted, but a more interesting tale says that a former lighthouse keeper who died in the lighthouse still haunts it. In a *Sun News* article of July 1987, Boatswain's Mate First Class Ken Marrow confirmed that "some funny things used to happen" at the lighthouse. He noted that many of the men stationed at the lighthouse claimed that "doors slammed shut, lights came on—all without explanation." Though not a part of history, it adds a bit of local color to the lonely, and now deserted, island.

Chapter 2

Prince Frederick's Episcopal Chapel

The Myth and Mystery of "Old Gunn" Church

Just outside of Georgetown is a landmark of great historical importance to South Carolinians, but oddly enough, finding information about historic Prince Frederick's Church can be a daunting task. One would think that trying to find out information about what was arguably the oldest church in the third-oldest city in the state would be easy, but while there are available bits of information here and there, other than a paragraph or two about its origins and a picture and mention of the historical marker located in front of the church's ruins, information about Prince Frederick's Church is scant.

However, try finding information about the site under the heading "Old Gunn" Church, and you can find everything from eyewitness accounts of hauntings to films purporting to show spirits and pictures claiming to show ectoplasmic entities. Ask someone in Georgetown where Prince Frederick's Chapel is, and in all likelihood you'll get a puzzled look in return; ask about Old Gunn, and you'll be directed to one of the most scenic and interesting ruins to be found along the upper South Carolina coast and perhaps anywhere in South Carolina. Prince Frederick's Church, once the meeting place of one of the most influential congregations in America and whose many parishioners were instrumental in the founding of our state and our nation, has all but been forgotten under its actual name and exists as a truly hidden part of our area history.

Prince Frederick Parish, named after the man who was then Prince of Wales, was formed by dividing Prince George Parish on April 9, 1734. The newly formed Prince Frederick Parish consisted of the land between the Black and Pee Dee Rivers and was the home of many of the area's most prosperous

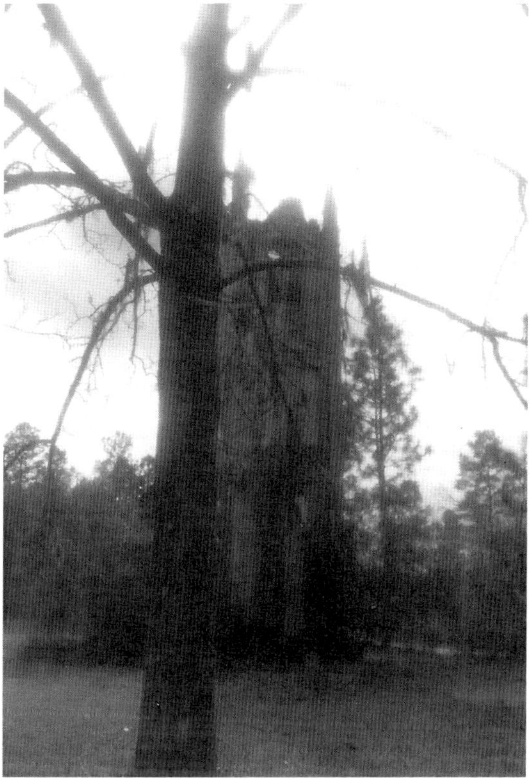

Right: The ruins of Prince Frederick's Episcopal Chapel. *Photograph by the author.*

Below and next page: These interior shots of the church bell tower illustrate the construction techniques used in the nineteenth century. *Photographs by the author.*

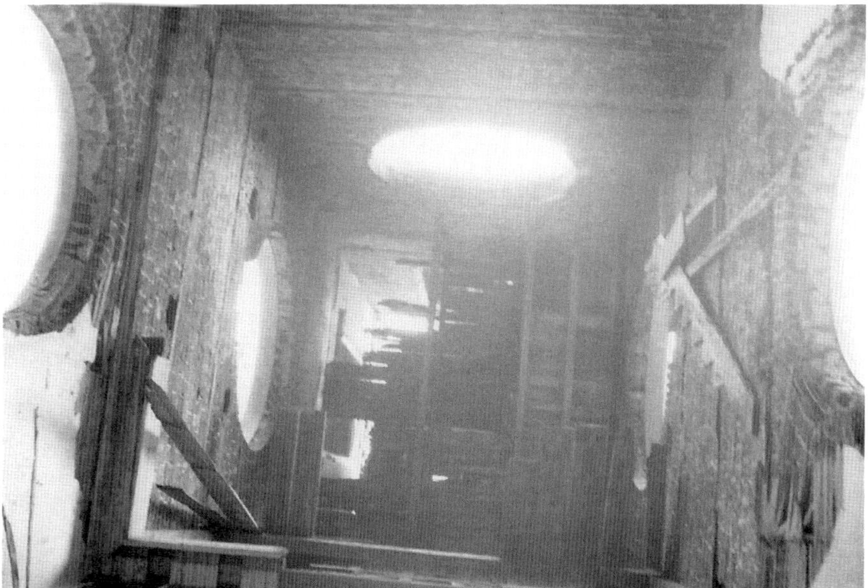

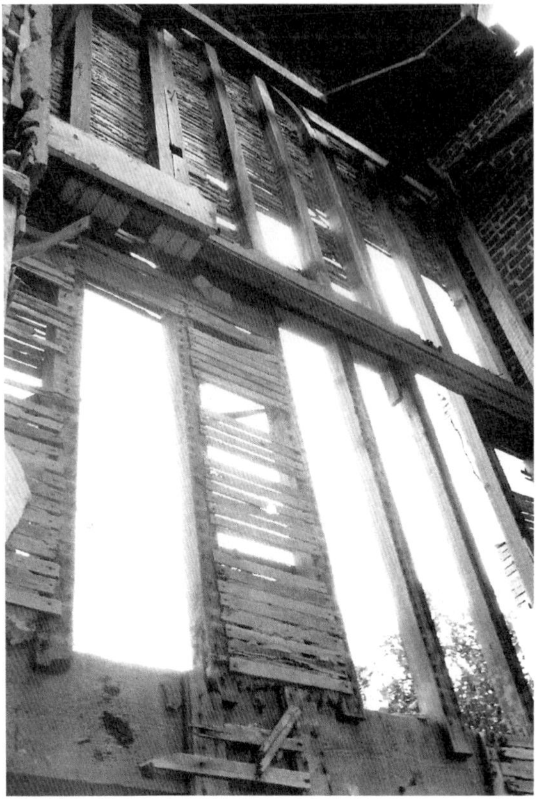

planters of rice, indigo and cotton. A church built in 1721 in what had been Prince George Parish was included in the area near the Black River that had been split off and then named Prince Frederick Parish, and this necessitated building a new church in Georgetown for Prince George Parish. Consequently, the city of Georgetown had a new and rather elaborate church, while the old wooden church standing in Prince Frederick Parish would continue to serve as both a house of worship and a meeting place for the residents of the new parish for many years.

With the agricultural boom that accompanied the rice-planting industry in the late eighteenth century, many of the parishioners of Prince Frederick Parish were among the wealthiest and most politically powerful people in America. For example, members of the congregation at Prince Frederick's church included men such as South Carolina delegate to the Continental Congress Thomas Lynch and South Carolina governor Joseph Alston during the church's early years, and South Carolina governor R.F.W. Allston would be a member during the nineteenth century. As a result, by 1835 the affluent congregation felt the need for a more fitting house of worship, especially since in Georgetown an English brick church built in Prince George Parish had opened by 1747 and, after having been burned down by British troops during the Revolutionary War, had been rebuilt better and even more impressively than before. The Reverend Hugh Fraser donated land on the Pee Dee for the construction of a new church in Prince Frederick Parish, and it was consecrated by the Reverend Nathaniel Brown in 1837. Even with the new church, within a few years the growing congregation dictated yet again

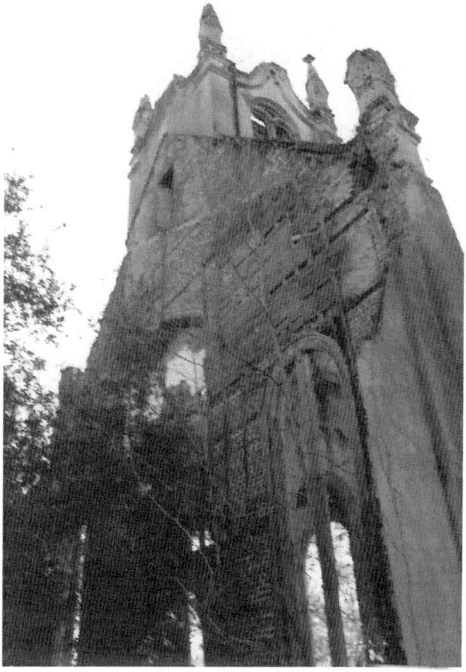

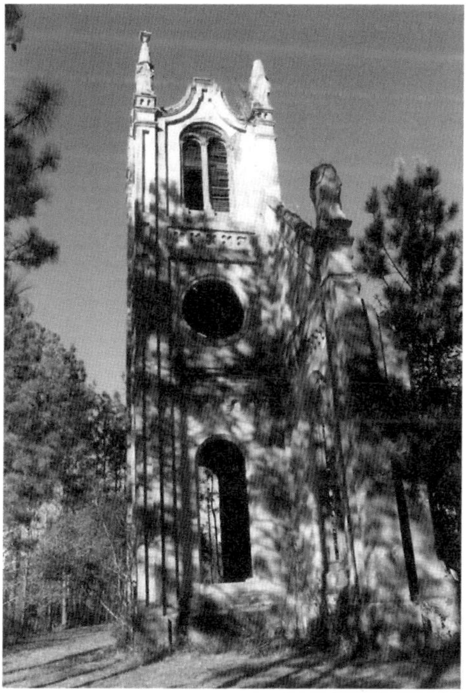

This page: These pictures of the church were taken in the late 1980s before the area was fenced off. *Photographs by the author.*

that the simple, newer church that had replaced the original did not meet the congregation's needs, and so in 1859 the most magnificent and grandest church of all began construction near Plantersville.

On November 17, 1859, former governor Robert F.W. Allston presided over the ceremony at which the cornerstone was laid for what was to be the new Gothic-style church. No expense was spared in selecting the adornments and furnishings for the church, and the affluent congregation saw to it that the finest furnishings that Europe had to offer were purchased and packed for shipping to America. But as the church neared completion, the residents of Prince Frederick's found themselves faced with a somewhat unique problem that prevented them from completing and using the church and installing the lush and expensive furnishings.

The Civil War had begun in 1861, and the ensuing Union blockade of the South had effectively prevented any of the luxurious furnishings intended for the church from reaching Prince Frederick Parish. Today, there is no record of what happened to the ship or its cargo. Even if the furnishings had arrived safely, by the time they arrived there would have been few area men who could have attended the church anyway. Most of the men in the area were members of the Tenth Regiment of South Carolina Volunteers, and during the war they fought and died at previously little-known places such as Murfreesboro, Chickamauga and Missionary Ridge. The ones who survived were still far from home, and their rice economy–based wealth was rapidly diminishing; so although work on the church continued for a while, by 1864 construction on the church stopped altogether due to lack of resources and a depleted congregation.

After the war, those few men lucky enough to return to the area found a parish that was now quite different. Most of the surviving rice planters, who had once been so influential and wealthy, now found themselves poor and destitute. The rice and indigo industry had almost completely collapsed with the abolition of slavery, and little of the planters' former lands or possessions remained, and most of the area plantations had been abandoned. With no money and few congregates, Prince Frederick's Parish church remained unfinished after the war, and though it was eventually finished in 1876, it remained sparsely furnished and certainly never achieved the level of opulence that was originally intended. It was used by a few residents to hold services for a while, but soon these dwindled to the point where the only service was held annually on Easter Sunday, when a visiting pastor would lead the scant congregation.

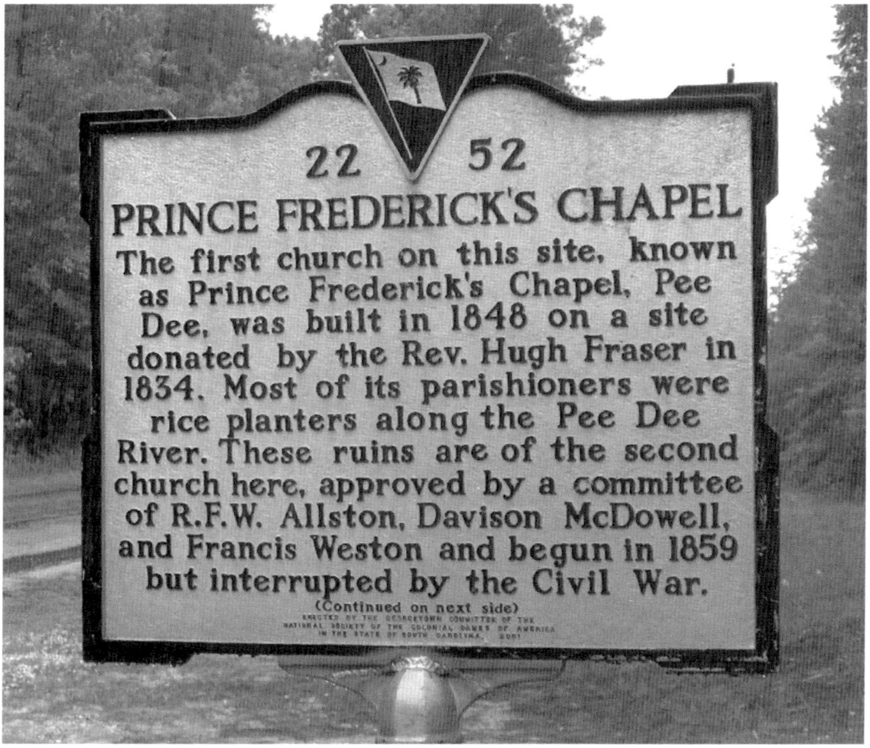

The Prince Frederick's historical marker in December 2009. *Photograph by the author.*

Eventually, just as the ways of the Old South died, so died Prince Frederick's. The church fell into a state of disrepair and ruin, and after a fire it was boarded up and condemned. In 1966, the church was demolished, save the bell tower and front wall, and only these two imposing ruins and the nearby graveyard remain today.

Unfortunately, over the last decade or so, the ruins have had to be fenced off with a high barbed wire fence to discourage souvenir (and especially ghost) hunters and graffitists. Consequently, though visitors can no longer enter the ruins themselves and take pictures, it is still possible to visit the site (there is a historical marker present) to view and photograph the magnificent ruins. Even today, those ruins hint at the grandeur of a once magnificent edifice that might be seen as a monument to the luxury and extravagancies of the Old South.

"Old Gunn" Church Mysteries

Of course, any building that has existed in some form for almost three hundred years, and one with as much history and tradition as Prince Frederick's, must have a ghost. Ironically, it is only because of this supposed haunting that the church has relevance for many people today. In fact, spirit-seeking visitors were no doubt responsible for the fences that now enclose the area, and the continued presence of teenagers looking for a thrill on moonlit nights made the crumbling ruins a place at which an accident may have been inevitable if the church had not been closed off. Many people, in fact, only know of the ruins at all because "Old Gunn" Church is said to be haunted.

According to legend, when the existing structure was being built in the early 1860s, the contractor for the project was a man known to us now only as Mr. Gunn. During the construction of the church, he supposedly fell to his death while working on the roof, and since that time the church has been recognized as one of the Grand Strand's most haunted landmarks. The ruins are said to be haunted in a variety of ways, but most commonly the ghost of Mr. Gunn is said to be seen walking around the belfry late on moonlit nights.

Over the years, legend has it that visitors to the site have reportedly heard ghostly choirs singing and seen ethereal figures moving around the graveyard. Though there is a lack of any concrete evidence of ghosts or any records to indicate that any part of the story is true, the remains of the church have become nearly legendary as a Halloween night retreat. Because of its remote location, the Prince Frederick's ghost is not as well known as other area spirits along the coast, such as Alice of the Hermitage or the Gray Man; however, the lasting influence of the ghost of Mr. Gunn can still be felt in that the church's name is tied more to the contractor than to the Prince of Wales.

The church at Prince Frederick's is without a doubt one of the Grand Strand's most interesting landmarks, despite the fact that it is in a remote location. Located on SC 22-4, off U.S. 701, about sixteen miles north of Georgetown, the ruins are not easy to find, but they are definitely worth a look for those who enjoy history, antebellum architecture or, perhaps, folklore and ghosts. In short, the Prince Frederick Parish Church is a truly hidden part of local history, and as such it has remained one of the area's most enduring, if isolated, attractions.

Chapter 3

The Sinking of the USS *Harvest Moon*

As one might expect, there have been many shipwrecks along the coast between Georgetown and Little River, and the fates of many have been recorded as far back as the Spanish ship *Capitana* in 1526. While these shipwrecks will be addressed in one comprehensive chapter in this work, the visible remains of just one of these wrecks still exists today. That ship has what is probably the most complete and interesting history, and as a result, the USS *Harvest Moon* deserves its own chapter in this book.

Like many ships that would take part in the American Civil War, the *Harvest Moon* did not begin its existence as a warship at all. However, unlike many other ships pressed into service, it was a newer ship and was actually launched by shipbuilder Joseph Dyer in Portland, Maine, on November 22, 1862. First owned by Spear, Lang and Delano of Boston, Massachusetts, the *Harvest Moon* was a ship of 546 tons and was 193 feet long, with a beam of 29 feet and an 8-foot draft. Its engines gave it a maximum speed of fifteen knots and an average speed of nine knots, and as a side-wheel steamer it had a vertical beam engine to power the wheel. Interestingly enough, the engine was actually salvaged from a steamer lost in the sea off China and then recovered and sent to Halifax, and perhaps superstitious individuals (as sailors are often wont to be) would have seen this as a bad omen in itself; as fate would have it, perhaps it was a bad omen indeed.

After a year in private service running passengers and freight between Bangor and Portland, the ship was purchased in Boston by Union commodore J.B. Montgomery for $99,300 and was fitted out as a ship of war. When commissioned on February 12, 1864, its armament consisted

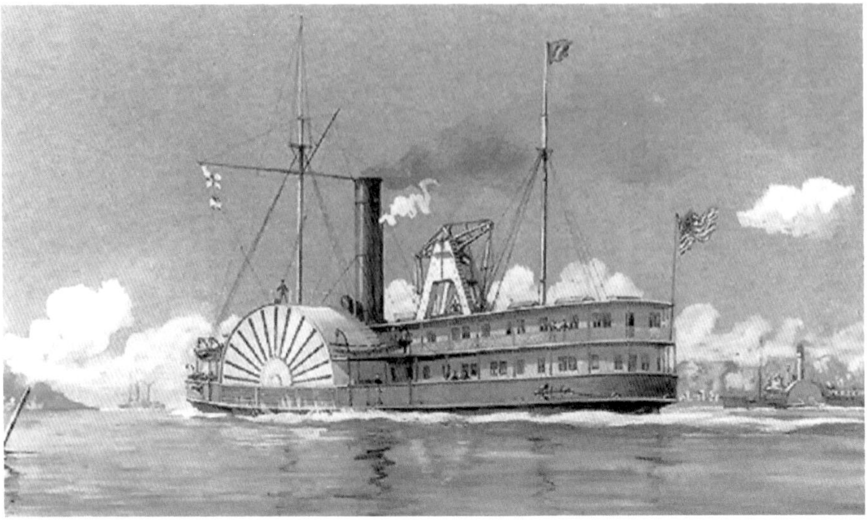

Official Records picture depicting the USS *Harvest Moon*. *Courtesy U.S. Navy Historical Center.*

of a twenty-pound Parrott rifle, four twenty-four-pound howitzers and one twelve-pound rifle. It was a rather graceful ship, and as such it was less suited for a gunboat because it had been built for service of another kind.

While in Union service, the *Harvest Moon* was an admiral's flagship, the admiral in this case being Rear Admiral John A. Dahlgren. Dahlgren was a career navy man and may be best known today for his fame as a naval ordnance innovator. Dahlgren invented a number of naval artillery pieces, and for his many innovations he has often been referred to as the "father of American naval ordnance." Dahlgren was given command of the South Atlantic Blockading Squadron in July 1863, and in this capacity his job was to blockade major southern ports, such as Charleston, and his command extended to Georgetown and its environs as well. Of his service as commander of the South Atlantic Blockading Squadron, the Naval Historical Center's biographies section notes that though Dahlgren was a brave and capable officer, his shortcoming was that "he never figured out how to counter the enemy's underwater defenses." This would be unfortunate for Dahlgren and the crew of the *Harvest Moon*.

Once commissioned and in the area encompassing Dahlgren's command, the *Harvest Moon* took station around Charleston. Almost immediately after being commissioned in February 1864, it seems that the ship had an inordinate number of discipline problems with the crew, and it seemed unlucky as well. In terms of the former, the captain's log noted a wide variety of disciplinary infractions just over the course of the first eight weeks of the ship's commission: March 4, "James McCue returned intoxicated and commenced breaking in 5 panels around the boiler. Confined in double irons"; March 20, "John Doyle (bargeman) was down in the main hold and took a hammock lashing without orders and when being spoken to by the Capt. was surly and was ordered confined in double irons"; March 26, "Thomas Tealy, carpenters mate confined for smuggling liquor thru the gate"; April 25, "Mustered all hands on quarter deck. Commenced searching baggage for $60 stolen from John B. Stanton, Marine. Found it concealed in clothing of William H. Morris (OS), confined in double. irons"; and April 26, "Confined Henry Quick dbl. irons. Presented forged pass at gate. 6 men AWOL." For such a new ship with a veteran crew, and an admiral's flagship at that, there seemed to be a high rate of infractions of a rather serious nature, from insubordination to theft and being absent without leave.

As for it being an unlucky ship, throughout what would be its brief career as a warship the *Harvest Moon* seemed to have the tendency to run into and over things. The first incident of note in the captain's log for March 2, 1864, notes that it "struck ground several times" and that "the ship [ran] on a mudbank." On March 16, the captain noted "at 4:15am saw a schooner…struck her on the starboard quarter. Captain & Exec. officer called immediately also all hands. the ship's bow was stove in making much water…6am 2 inches of water above keelson…All pumps going constantly to keep ship free. Passed Fort Washington and at 10:45 anchored. Stopped engine and ran donkey pump." For the next several days, the ship was pumped constantly in order to keep it afloat, and Admiral Dahlgren had to move his pennant to the USS *Baltimore* on March 19 until he deemed the *Harvest Moon* seaworthy on March 24.

Even more problematic was the ship's grounding a few months later on December 22, 1864, when it was stationed off Savannah. Its passenger that night was no less than General William T. Sherman, who was on board the *Harvest Moon* to conduct a council of war with Admiral Dahlgren. With his troops poised to take Savannah, Sherman had ordered his officers to make no moves while he was away. This was probably in order to keep overzealous officers from unadvisedly starting a major offensive, because certainly he could not have foreseen his delay in returning to his command. That night, when Sherman's conference with Dahlgren was over, the *Harvest Moon* became grounded in the mud once again and was unable to be moved until the following day. In the meantime, General William Hardee's Confederates were able to evacuate Savannah that same night, unwittingly aided by the fact that although the Federals were to some degree aware of the evacuation, they were powerless to pursue without explicit orders from Sherman. The next day, Hardee's men were gone, and as a result the grounding of the *Harvest Moon* had allowed thousands of Confederates to escape Savannah, free to fight another day. In a letter of January 1, 1865, to Chief of Staff General Henry Halleck, Sherman lamented the fact that the escape of Hardee's army, which he had hoped to trap and defeat, left him "very much disappointed." Once again, the unlucky *Harvest Moon*'s propensity to run onto things had led to disastrous results.

If a superstitious person needed anything else to make a case that the ship was unlucky, perhaps they might have pointed to the fact that its captain, John K. Crosby, had already had a date with infamy. Crosby had replaced the *Harvest Moon*'s first captain, Joshua Warren, and Crosby himself would probably be little more than a footnote in history were it not for his command before coming to the *Harvest Moon*. Crosby had been the master of the USS *Housatonic*, the Federal ship sunk by the Confederate submarine CSS *Hunley*. On the night of February 17, 1864, while anchored off the Charleston Bar, a lookout on the *Housatonic* spotted the *Hunley*. Crosby, who was on deck at the time, tried to get his ship underway but wasn't able to do so. In one of the most notable two-ship maritime encounters of the war—perhaps second only to the battle between the *Monitor* and the *Merrimac*—the *Hunley* rammed the *Housatonic* using a torpedo attached to a spar, and the *Housatonic* went down in minutes. The *Housatonic* became the first warship ever sunk by a submarine, and so Crosby was party to one of the most infamous firsts in Union naval history. Unfortunately for Crosby, it would not be the last time he would be commander of a ship that fell victim to a first of a rather dubious distinction.

By February 1865, however, the *Harvest Moon* seemed to have been riding a streak of good luck—albeit one of just a little more than a month's duration. The Confederacy was in shambles, and as the coastal ports and fortifications were being systematically gobbled up by the Union navy, their attention turned to one of the few remaining Confederate harbors on the coast—Winyah Bay and the port of Georgetown. Because Charleston had been the Union navy's main target on the South Carolina coast, it was only after it was secured that they were able to reassign the ships needed not just to blockade but also to actually subdue Georgetown. As far as the Federals were concerned, they probably felt that they would have to take the port by force, due to the presence of the largest military installation ever built on the Grand Strand: Battery White.

However, by the time Admiral Dahlgren and his men arrived on station in Georgetown on February 26, 1865, Battery White had already fallen. It had been abandoned by the fleeing Confederates as the remainder of the troops in Georgetown had been ordered to link up with General Joseph Johnston's army in North Carolina, and by the time Dahlgren arrived, the fort was occupied by a company of Federal marines. That same day, the town itself was garrisoned by six companies of Federal marines, and as he arrived Admiral Dahlgren proclaimed martial law in Georgetown—to which the officials of the town agreed as they subsequently surrendered the town. With the guns of the USS *Mingoe* trained on the town and the marines in place, Georgetown was under the flag of the United States of America for the first time in four years.

With the town under Federal control, the Union navy participated in a simple mop-up operation while trying to establish contact with Sherman's troops, who were closing in from the south. Admiral Dahlgren had amassed a considerable naval force in Winyah Bay, and during the last two weeks of February and up until the first of March—in addition to the *Harvest Moon* and the *Mingoe*—the USS *Catalpa*, USS *Chenango*, USS *Clover*, USS *Flambeau*, USS *Geranium*, USS *Mcdonough*, USS *Nipsic*, USS *Pawnee*, USS *Sonoma* and USS *Sweetbriar* were all stationed in and around Georgetown. Some of these ships explored the area's rivers, some stayed outside of the bar and some just waited so they would be on hand if any Confederate retaliation occurred. It was an impressive flotilla, and probably as a result few incidents of note had occurred since the *Harvest Moon* had been in port. Other than seeing lights on the shore, hearing an occasional rifle shot and having to open fire on a mysterious boat that may have been a drifting derelict, it was an uneventful time for the most part. Perhaps the only ill omen had been that on the twenty-seventh the *Harvest Moon* had run "onto a wreck off the city." Even when things were going the Union navy's way, the *Harvest Moon* had a tendency to hit things.

Early on the morning of March 1, Dahlgren ordered Crosby to get the ship underway and head back to Charleston, as his work was seemingly done in Georgetown. At about 7:45 am, as Dahlgren was having breakfast in his cabin, "a loud noise occurred and the bulkhead separating the cabin from the wardroom was shattered and driven in toward me…water was coming in through a great gap in the bottom. The main deck had also been blown through." Crosby claimed that he saw "a large hole, 10 feet by 12 feet square, stove through to the main deck fifteen to twenty feet aft of the shaft on the starboard side." At the time, no one was sure what had caused the explosion.

Ensign W.H. Bullis noted that he "felt a shock" and "seeing her smokestack shake I supposed her boiler had exploded." Engineer James A. Miller noted, "I experienced a shock and saw a column of water and smoke passing up through the deck some 14 feet from where I stood. My first impression was that a shell had exploded and I thought so until I reached the deck." Patrick McGrath, who was aft washing down the deck when he "was suddenly thrown overboard" by the explosion, claimed, "I thought a gun in the gangway had burst." Even Admiral Dahlgren was confused: "My first notion was that the boilers had burst; then the smell of burnt gunpowder suggested that the magazine had exploded." None of these assessments was correct, however. This time, the *Harvest Moon* had struck not a wreck or a sandbar but a "torpedo," or what would later come to be known as a floating mine.

The mine was not one that had been paddled up against the ship in the night, but rather a submerged mine that had been randomly planted in the bay before the *Harvest Moon* arrived. The previous fall, with the Federal push coming closer and closer to Georgetown, it was obvious that it was just a matter of time until the Union navy made an assault on Battery White and the surrounding area. There were no longer any blockade runners using Winyah Bay, so as a last line of defense, the decision had been made to mine the bay. This responsibility had fallen to Captain Thomas West Daggett of the First South Carolina Infantry, a Georgetown man who was by specialty an ordnance officer.

Daggett was well acquainted with the apparatus of building mines, and after deciding to mine Winyah Bay, he chose Stephen A. Rouquie to assist him. Rouquie had formerly been a lieutenant in the Tenth South Carolina Regiment Infantry but had resigned due to sickness in 1862; he later recovered and reenlisted with the German Artillery, which was then stationed at Battery White. By September, Daggett and Rouquie had constructed mines on the second floor of a store owned by the Rouquies on Front Street in Georgetown, and after the mines had been built, Daggett had them laid at strategic intervals in Winyah Bay, ready to detonate if struck by an invading Federal warship. Their work was not in vain, for the hole in the *Harvest Moon* was due to one of the water mines that Daggett and Rouquie had lain before the *Harvest Moon* arrived.

Union sympathizers among the residents of Georgetown had informed the Federals about the mines at least as early as January, but as Dahlgren noted, "So much has been said in ridicule of torpedoes that very little precautions are deemed necessary, and if resorted to are probably taken with less care than if due weight was attached to the existence of these mischievous things." Consequently, though there were later claims that the bay had recently been dragged for torpedoes by the *Mingoe*, somehow this one had been missed—even though it may have been in the bay for months. No matter how old the mine was, it did its job well, and the *Harvest Moon* went down in less than five minutes—by most accounts it sunk in less than two and a half minutes. Fred W. Racoe, acting third assistant engineer, testified that "in about 2 minutes the fireroom was full of water and the fires all out in the furnace. But it was only one half a minute from the time of the explosion that the fires were extinguished and the engine stopped." The *Harvest Moon* was literally dead in the water.

There was widespread panic after the explosion, and Dahlgren noted that

> *frightened men were struggling to lower the boats. I got by them with difficulty. They heard nothing; saw nothing. Passing from the gangway to the upper deck ladder, the open space was strewed with fragments of partitions. My foot went into some glass. The Fleet Captain was rushing down, and storming about. I ascended the ladder to get out on the upper deck to have a full view of things. A torpedo had been struck by poor old* Harvest Moon *and she was sinking.*

Fortunately, there were several Federal ships nearby, including the *Clover* and the *Pawnee*, and the men were evacuated quickly, as even Dahlgren realized that "there was no help for it, so we prepared to leave the vessel." Unbelievably, there was only one casualty, wardroom steward John Hazard, whose body was found the next day. It went down in two and a half fathoms of water—a depth of about fifteen feet—perhaps contributing to the low casualty count, the rapidity with which it sank and the success with which the Federals would salvage everything usable from the ship. As a result, Crosby noted that even after it came to rest on the bottom, the "the spar and hurricane deck was above water, and the gun deck [was just] one foot under water."

Immediately, the other Federal ships sent boats out to drag the area for torpedoes, but no more were ever found, and so it was as if the hapless and unlucky *Harvest Moon* had hit the one remaining torpedo in all of Winyah Bay. The other Union ships posted an armed guard on the wreck—easy to do since its uppermost decks were above water—to keep any lingering Confederates from attempting to salvage anything usable from the ship. Over the next few days, the Federals had "all hands employed in unrigging ship unbinding sails…Engineers and Firemen employed in removing the machinery from the ship." The crew also removed any stores they could, even beef and pork stored in the hold. After removing the chains, anchors and every piece of usable machinery, the wreck was officially abandoned on April 21, 1865. By that time, the war was over, and though just a few weeks earlier efforts may have been made to raise the ship as it was, in such shallow water, it was allowed to remain there, where it rests to this day.

A subsequent board of inquiry returned a verdict of "sunk by torpedo, no blame," noting that

> [t]*here being no more required evidence the court, after due consideration, report the following facts: That the USS Harvest Moon, having the flag of Rear Admiral John Dahlgren was accidentally sunk by a torpedo placed in the Marsh Channel, Winyah Bay, South Carolina, on the first day of March 1865. That we fully and entirely exculpate from blame all on board said vessel at the time of the catastrophe there being no possible chance under the circumstances shown in the testimony of saving the vessel or preventing her from sinking.*

Had the *Harvest Moon* gone down earlier in the war, no doubt it would have been salvaged and would have seen service once again, but by the time it was stripped and ready to begin any operation to raise it, the war was over, and Reconstruction became the focus of the Federal occupying forces in and around Georgetown. Thus, the *Harvest Moon* rested forgotten on the bottom in Winyah Bay, and over the years the ship settled farther down into the alluvial mud, and storms—including a number of major hurricanes—and sea waves raised the level of the mud as well. By the mid-1960s, roughly one hundred years after its sinking, it was estimated that perhaps six feet of mud covered its top decks. Only its boiler stack still remained visible above the water.

During the 1960s, several enterprising groups and individuals began to show an interest in the *Harvest Moon*. In 1963, an expedition from the New England Naval and Maritime Museum began examining the wreck and determined that at that time the vessel was in extremely good condition. Another group called the Southern Explorations Association reportedly considered raising the *Harvest Moon* as a tourist attraction to serve in conjunction with a planned maritime museum on Front Street. There was a call for investors and apparently even talk of putting a World War II submarine periscope in the museum that afforded a view of the bay, but eventually this idea fell through as well. All this time, however, it was officially a U.S. Navy ship, and only in February 1963 did Assistant Secretary of the Navy Kenneth E. BeLieu sign the document

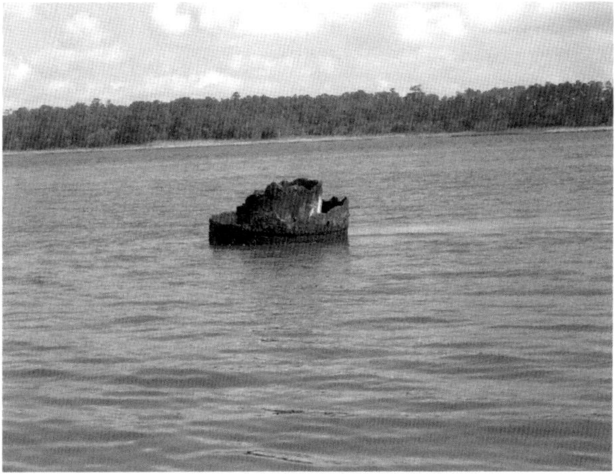

Right: A close-up of the boiler stack of the *Harvest Moon* as seen today. *Courtesy Scott Lawrence.*

Below: Official U.S. Navy photo that shows divers examining the *Harvest Moon* in 1963. *Courtesy U.S. Navy Historical Center.*

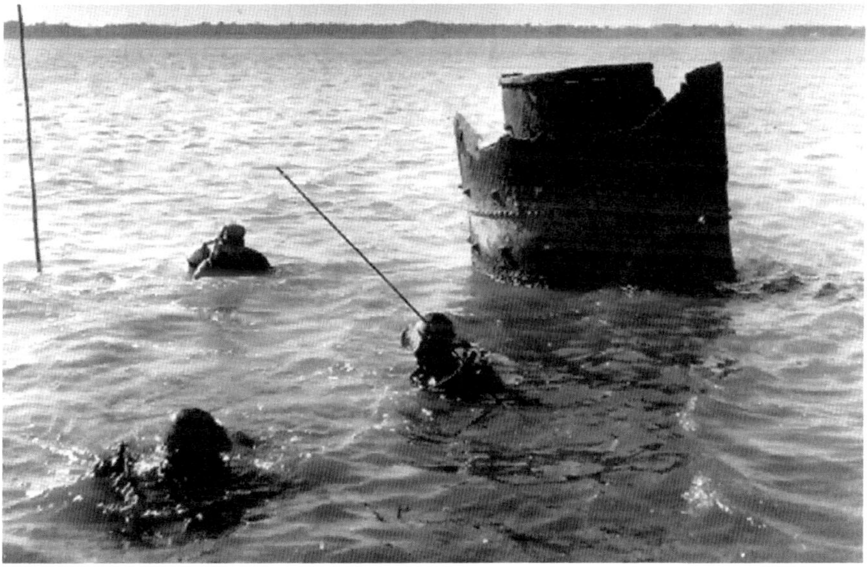

that granted the ship its release from the navy and allowed interested parties to salvage it if they desired. To date, that still hasn't happened, and in all likelihood that becomes less likely with each passing year.

Even today, all one needs is a boat with a very shallow draft (nautical charts mark the depth of the water around the boiler of the *Harvest Moon* as being from one to four feet), the right tide and a spirit of adventure, and you can take a trip out into Winyah Bay and touch the old boiler sticking up out of the water, all that remains of a once great, if unlucky, ship.

Chapter 4

The History of Battery White

Because of the ever-changing nature of the South Carolina coastline, only a few Grand Strand sites of historical interest have survived into the twenty-first century. Shipwrecks have been covered by shifting sands, a number of structures have fallen victim to hurricanes and many sites that might today be seen as historically relevant were often razed or built over because the land they were on was too valuable to let sit. Consequently, one thing that many area historical sites have in common is that they simply no longer exist as they once did. In some rare cases, however, such as Battery White, the site has been spared the ravages of time and tourism to some extent and remains in a form viewable by us today. Though it is no longer the one-hundred-acre fort it was in 1865—marked by a small wooden sign, a granite marker and two cannons—the remaining earthworks give us a pretty good idea of the "well placed, well constructed, and strongly armed" fortress that Union admiral John Dahlgren saw in 1865.

Oddly enough, unlike Confederate forts built on North Island, South Island and Cat Island, at Little River and at Murrells Inlet, Battery White was not built early in the war. By 1861, there were forts defending Georgetown at the mouths of the North and South Santee Rivers and on North Island, South Island and Cat Island because Confederate officials believed that South Carolina would be invaded either at Hilton Head or Georgetown because the Union navy wanted a safe anchorage within striking distance of Charleston. Winyah Bay was not only large enough to harbor the entire United States Navy in 1861, but it also provided access to the Black, Pee Dee, Waccamaw and Sampit Rivers. In Georgetown, Colonel Arthur Middleton

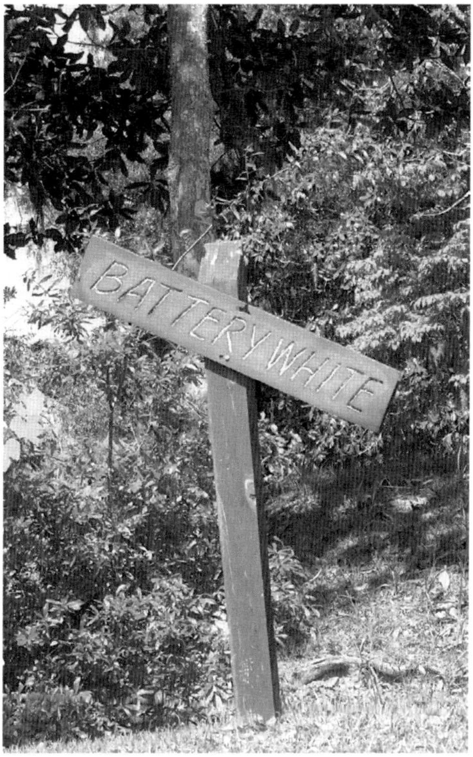

A wooden sign today marks the site of Battery White. *Courtesy Scott Lawrence.*

Manigault, a local man who owned a plantation on the Santee, was in charge of the area then known as the First Military District, and as such he had nearly three thousand men at his disposal. However, after the Federals invaded and captured Hilton Head in November 1861, Manigault's force was reduced to one thousand men by December.

On March 14, 1862, Brigadier General John C. Pemberton was placed in overall command of the district, and one of his first decisions was to strip the area defenses and concentrate the majority of his available forces in Charleston. He wrote to Colonel Manigault on March 25, stating, "Having maturely considered the subject, I have determined to withdraw the forces from Georgetown, and therefore to abandon the position…You will proceed with all the infantry force under your command to this city, Charleston, and report to Brigadier General Ripley." Colonel Manigault was appalled. In addition to the largest regiment of infantry in the district, the Tenth South Carolina, he was to remove most of the cavalry, all of the guns and ordnance stores and, in essence, everything of military value. The man who succeeded Manigault as commander of the First District, Colonel Robert F. Graham of the Twenty-first South Carolina, was to remain in Georgetown with his troops, but by April 10 they would be transferred out as well. With the exception of the locally raised Waccamaw Light Artillery and a couple of companies of the state troops that would later become part of the Fourth and Seventh South Carolina Cavalries, the district was virtually undefended by mid-April 1862.

In addition to the troop withdrawals, most of the area forts, all of which were finished or nearly finished, were abandoned and left ungarrisoned.

The forts had their guns removed and replaced with painted logs, called "Quaker" guns, so that it at least appeared that the installations were still heavily fortified. Eventually, twenty guns from the district forts were removed and sent up the Pee Dee River to the Northeastern Bridge, at which time they were transferred to railroad cars and shipped to Charleston.

As Colonel Manigault knew, it was a drastic decision and an impossible task for the few remaining troops. He later wrote:

> *So far as General Pemberton's orders applied to myself and my regiment, I did not regret the change, for we were all anxious for one…but knowing his intention as to the abandonment of this most productive grain-growing country, believing that its loss would be very seriously felt by the Confederacy in one way or another, and knowing that the destruction of the batteries and the removal of the troops would prove an invitation to the enemy too strong and too important to be resisted, the whole country lying at the mercy of a single gunboat, I took leave of my old district rather low in spirits, and with a strong presentment of coming evil.*

It didn't take the Federals long to grasp the situation, and they soon took action. Colonel Manigault, who was by then far from Georgetown, later heard about conditions in Georgetown and wrote that, just as he had believed in April,

> [w]*hoever occupied Georgetown had control of these rivers as well as the Santee River to some degree, meaning that the possessor had a great degree of control in South Carolina. For that reason, it should have come as no surprise when the Federal Navy began to probe upriver, giving many area troops their first real taste of what was to come. My forebodings were soon verified. A few weeks after we left, two U.S. gunboats entered the bay, and proceeded to Georgetown and up the neighboring rivers, and carried off many Negroes, destroyed much property, and created great alarm. These visits were repeated several times, and on the Santees like raids were undertaken by the enemy. Those of the planters who were able to do so removed their Negroes and such property as could conveniently be transported into the interior or out of reach of the enemy, their plantations abandoned and the growing crops left to perish in the fields.*

The first of these Union forays into the area took place on May 21, 1862. On that date, the USS *Albatross*, commanded by George A. Prentiss, and the USS *Norwich*, commanded by Lieutenant J.M. Duncan, entered Winyah Bay. Passing North Island, they noted that the redoubt and lighthouse were deserted but that they could see "on South Island quite an extensive fortification, with apparently several large guns mounted en barbette." Upon approaching the fort, they saw that it was deserted and that the cannons were actually the Quaker guns. From South Island, they could see that the Cat Island fort had been deserted and armed with Quaker guns as well. Knowing now that the bay was undefended, on May 22, the *Albatross* and the *Norwich* steamed into Georgetown.

As the Union ships approached the wharves, their "guns within 30 yards of the houses," Confederate major William P. Emmanuel, who had succeeded Graham and was now temporarily in command of the district, had his men set fire to the turpentine-laden brig *Joseph* and set it adrift. This attempt to drive back the Union ships failed, and the Federal ships approached the town unimpeded. Surprisingly, no exchange of gunfire took place, even with both forces in such proximity to each other, but both commanders had excellent reasons for holding their men in check. Major Emmanuel knew that he was "not prepared to offer them an effectual resistance while they remain[ed] on their boats," and Commander Prentiss felt that "a contest in the streets would have compelled me to destroy the city, involving the ruin of the innocent with the guilty." Later that afternoon, the two Union ships went about ten miles up the Waccamaw River and raided a mill, carrying off eighty slaves in the process.

Soon, the Federals occupied or destroyed the forts that the Confederates had abandoned, which gave them control of and access to Winyah Bay, Georgetown, and the neighboring rivers. Already, it was all too obvious that Pemberton's stripping of the Confederate defenses in the area had been a grievous error. The Confederate high command recognized the gravity of this error, and by August 3, General Pemberton himself visited Georgetown to select a site on which to build new forts that would defend Georgetown and block the access to all of the area's rivers. Since the original forts on North, South and Cat Islands were now in Federal possession, Pemberton selected Mayrants Bluff and Frazier's Point for the site of the new forts. These two positions were located across the bay from each other, and as such any Federal ships attempting to enter the lower bay once the forts were completed would be caught in a murderous crossfire. Additionally, plans were made to strengthen the interior defenses along the major rivers while the large forts were being built, and this would hopefully enable the planters to reach a level of productivity unseen since the Federals began patrolling the rivers.

The area residents, especially the plantation owners, couldn't see the forts built fast enough. Even South Carolina governmental officials were clamoring for help, as the planters made up a large and influential block of wealthy voters. One move that made the local citizenry happy was when General Pemberton was promoted to lieutenant general and sent west to command the department of Mississippi, and in his stead General P.G.T. Beauregard was placed in command of the department of South Carolina, Georgia and Florida. Beauregard was well liked in South Carolina, and he certainly knew how to deal with local officials more tactfully than had the irascible Pemberton. Beauregard wrote to Governor Francis Pickens on October 8, 1862, about the state of affairs around Georgetown and assured Pickens that he had "already given orders for the construction of a battery of five or six pieces of artillery (32 pounders and rifled guns) at Mayrant's, for the defense of Winyah Bay." He noted, however, that he would only be able to garrison it with 350 men, but considering the situation in Georgetown, this would have been more than welcome.

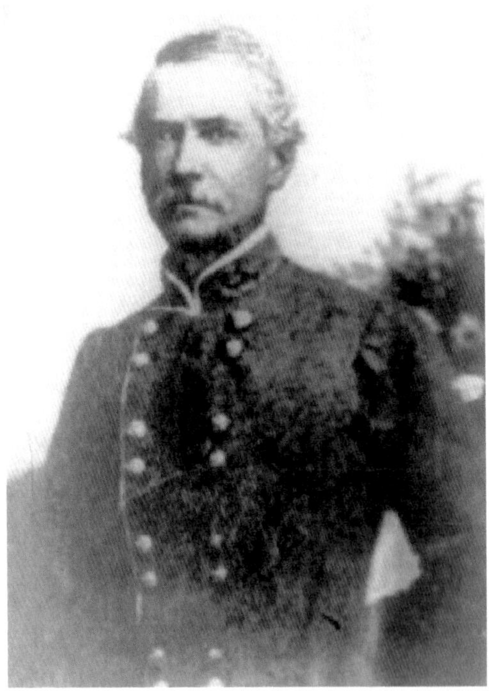

Confederate General James Heyward Trapier, Georgetown native, served the district capably during the years he was stationed in the area. He is buried at Prince George Church in Georgetown. *Courtesy Library of Congress.*

Assessing the situation in the Horry-Georgetown district, Beauregard decided that it was necessary to place an officer in charge who would carry enough clout to unite the many independent companies of cavalry and artillery stationed in the district and enable them to operate effectively in concert. Beauregard decided to give the command of the area to a man who was not only a friend and West Point classmate of his, but also one familiar with the local people and the region. The man Beauregard selected was Brigadier General James Heyward Trapier, a native of Georgetown.

General Trapier had been born at Windsor Plantation on

the Black River in 1815, and although he had graduated from West Point third in the class of 1838 (Beauregard had graduated second), he had shown little military aptitude to confirm his high standing at such a respected military school. But Beauregard felt that Trapier was well suited for the job he had in mind, and in fact Trapier would prove to be quite capable, serving in the area almost for the remainder of the war. Upon his arrival, however, Trapier was discouraged by conditions in the district. He soon found that he had fewer than six hundred men in his command, and many of these were the sick and walking wounded.

Almost immediately, Trapier began pleading for additional troops and would do so for the remainder of the war. In fact, almost every extant letter written by Trapier to his superiors is filled with pleas for more troops, artillery and supplies. He was able to get a company of the Second South Carolina Artillery under the command of Captain Frederick F. Warley, plus a company of cavalry, to garrison the fort being built at Mayrants Bluff. These troops did most of the construction work on the fort at night on the advice of General Thomas Jordan, Confederate chief of staff, who wrote on October 19 that "sham works should be attempted at some point while in view of the [Federal] gunboats, and meanwhile the real works should be vigorously prosecuted at night."

The Federals weren't fooled, however, and on November 11, two Federal gunboats started firing on the fort, and Captain Warley's men returned their fire with the nine pieces of artillery by then mounted in the fort. After a few minutes, the Federals retired, but it was by now apparent to all that the Federals were aware of the work being done at that site. On November 21, Federal naval commander J.C. Beaumont of the USS *Sebago* had noted that construction was underway at Mayrants Bluff and that he had been informed that more artillery pieces were expected soon. There were two things Trapier's new fort didn't have, however: enough men to properly man it and the large guns he felt he would need to fight off a full-scale Union attack.

General Beauregard had written to Colonel James Chestnut in Columbia on November 10 and ordered a regiment of state troops to Trapier's position to man the "batteries until other forces can be sent in that direction." Even desperate for troops, however, Trapier was appalled at the state militia he was sent. On November 17, Trapier noted that they "arrived without arms and without ammunition. These troops are, besides, Reserves, and in service for only ninety days. It is questionable whether they can be rendered efficient in that time, even if well armed and equipped. At present they are literally worth nothing at all." Beauregard replied to Trapier that he would send him the arms and ammunition but that those were the only troops he could spare.

Trapier also wanted big guns—Columbiads. Beauregard wrote to Trapier in December saying that he agreed he could use the guns and that he had approved his application but, unfortunately, that no such guns were available. What Beauregard got, instead, was rhetoric from his superiors, to the effect that he would be better served to construct "detached batteries of two or three guns, well protected by traverses, so as to form a separate chamber for each gun, and the batteries 100 or 200 yards apart." Trapier was to be sent "two light pieces, to be put in position on Frazier's Point, opposite Mayrant's Bluff. One 12 pounder smoothbore and one rifled gun (Blakely) both on siege carriages have been ordered." In other words, Trapier wasn't going to get the Columbiads, and he would have to make do with fieldpieces instead.

Trapier had ordered the Waccamaw Light Artillery posted at Frazier's Point, where it was initially planned that a sister fort to the one on Mayrants Bluff be built, but construction was halted at some point in order to finish the one at Mayrants Bluff first. The Mayrants Bluff position was more or less complete by February 1863 and had been designated Battery White. On February 3, Trapier reported that Warley's fifty-three men were there manning nine guns and that the Waccamaw Light Artillery was stationed at the Frazier's Point earthworks with the fieldpieces. Although these troops were thinly spread, it was hoped that with the addition of the armament at Battery White the Federals would cease their forays up the area rivers—in that case perhaps some of the planters who had fled the area would return and once again begin producing the rice that was so vital to the undernourished Confederacy. But as General Manigault later wrote, it was too little, too late:

> *A certain amount of protection was thus again secured to the planters, but the mistake, excepting to a very limited extent, could not be corrected.* [They]…*lost much confidence in the wisdom of the military authorities, and not knowing how soon again they might have to flee*…[the] *system of labor which had hitherto existed in the cultivation of these valuable plantations could not be restored. They ceased to be productive, barely making a sufficiency for the labourers themselves. In this way, a very considerable portion of our labouring population, instead of producing as they might have done, a large amount of subsistence for our soldiers in the field, besides supplying themselves, had to be provided for from other portions of the state, at a time when the country could ill afford to spare anything in*

> *the way of food. This instance is only one of many where mismanagement on the part of the Government or its officials, by sacrificing their resources and multiplying their incumbrances, contributed to our final failure.*

General Trapier knew that no matter how brave his men were, the vast amount of Federal manpower available would eventually overwhelm his troops unless he received some reinforcements. Despite appearances, Battery White was as yet without adequate firepower or troops to defend Georgetown. Although there were, by January, eleven pieces of artillery in the fort, none of the guns was large and all were insufficient if called on to deal with ironclads. Furthermore, the gunboat CSS *Pee Dee* was nearing completion at the Confederate navy yard upriver at Mars Bluff, and if the Federals succeeded in capturing Battery White, they would easily be able to ascend to the navy yard and destroy the *Pee Dee* before it was completed. To emphasize the need for more troops and artillery, Trapier wrote to his headquarters in Charleston on January 26. Trapier claimed that Battery White was insufficient to defend even upper Winyah Bay, much less the nearby rivers. To add further weight to his argument, he stated:

> *The Confederate navy-yard at Mars Bluff, Peedee River is assuming daily greater and greater importance. Already has there been nearly completed there a vessel of war of some magnitude…It is contemplated, as I learn, to build others, and it seems probable that important additions to our Navy will continue to be supplied from this yard as long as the war may last… its growing importance will naturally attract the attention of the enemy. It is my duty, therefore, to invite attention to the fact that the only defense for this navy-yard consists in the battery which guards the entrance to Winyah Bay…I need not refer to the armament of Battery White; the commanding general is of course aware of its weakness…I hope I shall not be considered importunate in thus again inviting the attention of the commanding general to the subject. To me it seems of no mean importance.*

Instead of reinforcements, though, Trapier was to yet again lose troops. On February 1, Trapier noted the desertions of the Third and Fourth South Carolina state troops, under the command of Lieutenant Colonel R.A. Rouse and Colonel J.H. Witherspoon. These men declared that their term of enlistment was up, and as such, they were free to go. On February 17, Trapier wrote to Beauregard lamenting conditions in the district, noting that he now had only about three hundred men in his command, and spread out over sixty miles of coastline, they would be ineffective if needed to repel a Federal invasion.

In fact, Trapier had been losing troops at an alarming rate during the previous nine months. Captain Tucker's company of independent cavalry had been made Company F of the regular Seventh South Carolina Cavalry and was sent to Virginia on March 18. In March, he also lost the two companies of the Twenty-first Georgia Cavalry, which had been stationed in Murrells Inlet. Company D of the Second South Carolina Artillery had already been transferred, but at least it would be replaced by Company B of the German Artillery in May 1863.

Trapier was even more concerned than usual about the diminution of troops because, at the same time, the Union navy was getting more and more aggressive. On January 19, three Union ships were spotted patrolling just below Battery White, and by March they were doing more than patrolling. On March 2, the Union navy landed some men below Battery White and pushed back the Confederate pickets. They pressed the issue no further, however, and this brief reconnaissance only served to agitate Trapier more—he felt that it may have been made with "a view to ulterior operations." Within days, he renewed his requests for more troops and artillery.

Trapier wanted infantry, and he wanted three ten-inch Columbiads. Columbiads were large artillery pieces used mainly in seacoast fortifications such as Battery White. They were formidable guns—ten caliber, a projectile weight of 128 pounds and with a range of over 1,800 yards. Trapier believed that with the Columbiads, Battery White could withstand any assault that the Union navy might mount. On March 8, he wrote that Battery White, though, was "well-constructed and of ample dimensions [but] feebly armed":

> *It is well situated, too, at the gorge which divides the upper from lower Winyah Bay, where the width of the channel does not exceed 1400 yards. Its site likewise is commanding, having some 20 feet elevation above the ordinary high water, but were it Gibraltar, it would be useless in a conflict with plated vessels, armed as it is at present…experience has demonstrated that against ironclads it would simply be a waste of ammunition to contend with such guns as these…we want the 10-inch Columbiad. Give us but three of these, and so far as the water approach is concerned, this section of the country will have adequate protection.*

Trapier wasn't finished, however, and of course he wanted troops, too. "One thousand men behind the intrenchments which have been constructed would be more than a match for five times their number. Is not the saving of the district from the hands of the enemy worth three 10-inch guns and one regiment of infantry?" he asked. The guns weren't forthcoming, and again on March 13 he even asked the authorities in Richmond for the guns, but again he was denied. A report of May 1864 shows the armament at Battery White to be a thirty-two-pound smoothbore, one twelve-pound smoothbore, six twenty-four-pound smoothbores, one six-pound smoothbore, three thirty-two-pound rifles, three twelve-pound rifles and one 3½-inch Blakely—but, again, no Columbiads. The Waccamaw Light Artillery had three six-pounders and one 3½-inch Blakely in place at the unfinished earthworks and trenches on Frazier's Point.

Trapier was becoming increasingly frustrated, as he seemed to lose more and more cavalry and receive a few less-mobile artillerymen in return. This lack of troops and his rapidly shrinking forces prompted him to write to Confederate chief of staff Brigadier General Thomas Jordan on March 27:

> *Under these circumstances it is obvious that a portion of the district may of necessity be abandoned to the enemy. The question arises, which shall it be? The center of the position (Winyah Bay) must of course be held; to abandon it would of course be tantamount to the abandonment of the whole. If we withdrew from Waccamaw Neck, we would throw open wide the entire line of coast from Winyah Bay to the North Carolina line. There will not be so much as a sentinel throughout the entire extent…There is a very great danger that the navigation of the Pedee and Waccamaw Rivers will be obstructed by field batteries held in the vicinity of the latter. Again the Navy Yard at Mars Bluff would, in the event of the abandonment of Waccamaw Neck, be entirely uncovered.*

At this point in the war, though, it was getting hard to hold on to the men he had, even if they weren't siphoned off to another department. On October 5, 1864, Lieutenant R.P. Swann of the USS *Potomska* reported to Rear Admiral John A. Dahlgren that he had "11 privates, Company B, German Artillery, who deserted from Battery White…the deserters report great dissatisfaction among the troops, particularly the Germans, who say they would desert without an exception were they not so strictly guarded. I find the river so strongly picketed that I can give them little assistance." Swann went on to give exact information about the battery and guns there, noting that "at Battery White there are ten guns…in the rear of the battery there is a section artillery consisting of two rifled 12-pounders."

The mention of the two guns at the rear was the first mention of what was apparently designated Fort Wool by the Confederates, a second fortified position under construction that would have controlled the ground to the rear of Battery White. Swann's information regarding the deployment of troops was quite explicit as well, and he noted that "two companies of Cavalry, commanded by Captains Kirk and Walker, are directly in the rear of Battery White…there are…two companies of cavalry on Waccamaw Neck" and that "400 men encamped 6 miles from the town." Trapier did seem, at last, to have a fair-sized contingent in Georgetown, though certainly not enough to repel a major invasion.

By November, Sherman's armies were advancing at an alarming rate. The same companies of artillery and cavalry that had been in the district all summer were still on duty, but one by one they would begin to be transferred out. Trapier now had 361 men and 22 officers, but Kirk's Rangers were gone by the nineteenth. Gaillard's Artillery also left on the nineteenth. In fact, by November 23, only Company B of the German Artillery was left to defend the district. Trapier himself was ordered out, so by the first of the year the highest-ranking officer in the district was Lieutenant Hermann Klatte, now commanding the German Artillery in Battery White.

Lieutenant Klatte had been ordered to hold out as long as possible and then withdraw. Although now only one company of artillery was left to defend the entire district, those men were stationed at the most crucial point as far as access to the waterways was concerned. Battery White still presented the Federals with a formidable obstacle, because at long last Trapier had indeed received two much-coveted ten-inch Columbiads, the large defensive guns that would make Battery White well-nigh impregnable. But even the Columbiads came too late. After the fall of Charleston on February 17, 1865, all major Southern ports were in the hands of Federal forces. Though Georgetown was hardly on par with Wilmington or Charleston, it was nevertheless the last large port in Confederate hands in South Carolina and, for that matter, one of very few left in the Confederacy. The Federals quickly moved to mount an operation to take Georgetown, and just as quickly the Confederates chose to abandon the position.

On February 20, with Union forces closing in by land and by sea, Lieutenant Klatte and the German Artillery finally evacuated Battery White, and the people of Georgetown were left to their own devices. In the meantime, Union commander J. Blakely Creighton took the USS *Mingoe* to within a mile and a half of Battery White and then sent out boats to check for mines before proceeding. After finding no mines, Creighton brought his ship up close to the fort and fired several rounds into the compound. Confederate deserters had told the Federals that the fort was now abandoned, so Creighton expected no response—and he got none.

Creighton next sent a landing party to the fort to confirm that it was completely deserted. Executive Officer J.W. Congdon led this party, and he soon reported back to Creighton that the fort was indeed abandoned. Congdon also reported that all fifteen of the artillery pieces had been spiked and rendered unusable (in a second report, he claimed that there were sixteen guns) and that there were massive quantities of shot and shell but no gunpowder. Creighton noted that the fort was "well-constructed, and very formidable" and that his men "dismantled it by dismounting the guns, [and] breaking the carriages." He stationed a company of fifty

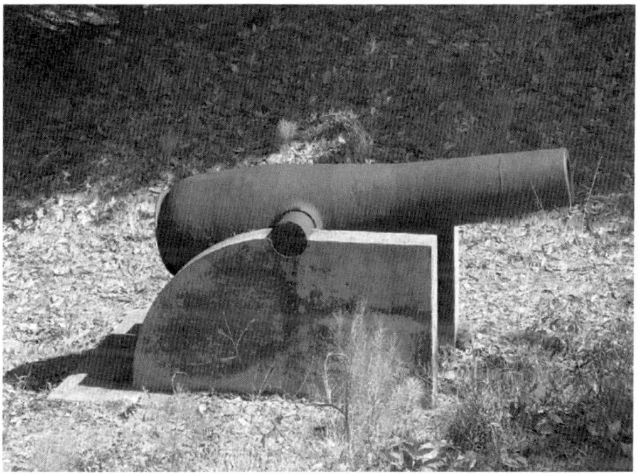

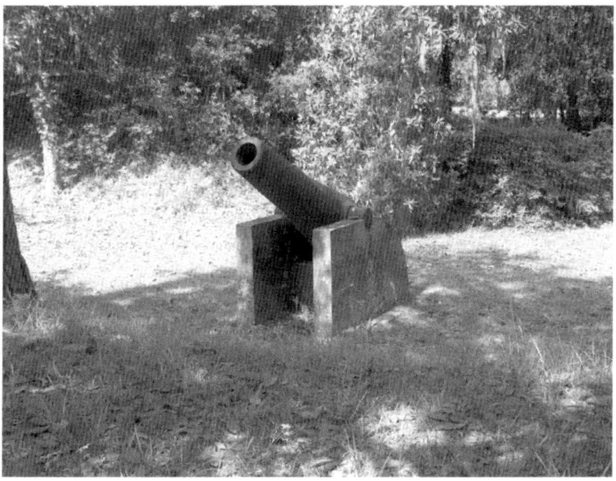

This page: The two ten-inch Columbiads that General Trapier worked so hard to get were never used to defend the battery, as they arrived too late in the war. Both are still there today. *Courtesy Scott Lawrence.*

marines under Lieutenant S.L. Breese in the fort and then contacted Dahlgren with his findings.

On the twenty-fifth, Georgetown surrendered, and the town was occupied by six companies of marines under Lieutenant George Stoddard. On the twenty-sixth, Dahlgren himself arrived and declared martial law. The war was over for Georgetown and Battery White.

On February 28, Dahlgren finally took the opportunity to see for himself the fort that the Federals had been so curious about, and he was impressed by what he saw:

> *Generally it has been much underrated, but we can now understand it was well placed, well constructed, and strongly armed, so we should have had some trouble to reduce it if well manned. The accounts in the reports fail to convey a correct idea of its character. The site was admirably selected, not only commanding the channel, but the various roads to the town above. The principal battery looks directly on the water, well planned and executed carefully, not only with reference to a cannonade by ships, but also to assault from the water.*

Dahlgren went on to explain that there were many "admirably contrived huts…capable of holding a considerable force," as well as "ranges of stalls for horses." Dahlgren noted also that the habitations were dry and even had brick chimneys. "The whole site would have held a couple of thousand men easily," he wrote, "and our 50 marines were hardly noticeable" in an area that Dahlgren noted enclosed a "space occupied by all might [of] about 100 acres."

The armament in the main battery was impressive. "Three 32-pounder (6.4 inches) rifles (hooped), 2 X-inch columbiads, 4 24-pounders (smooth), 2 12-pounders rifled (hooped), 1 3 3/4 inch (smooth)…One 24-pounder (smooth), 1 12 pounder (smooth)" wrote Lieutenant E.O. Matthews on the twenty-fourth. This gave Battery White a total of sixteen guns. "The whole position was so strong that, if defended by the 500 men said to have been there," Dahlgren wrote, "we should have found it a tough business, even with the force I proposed, and it is doubtful that we could have forced the rear line." Dahlgren came to the conclusion that "it is doubtful that a strong naval force could have taken it without an ironclad and a land force in reverse."

It seems that Trapier's fortification had become the near-impregnable bastion that he had envisioned, right down to the long-awaited ten-inch Columbiads. Dahlgren seemed to confirm that, had Trapier been given the men he desired, it would have taken a long and bloody siege to subdue Battery White. Yet quickly, painlessly and bloodlessly, Battery White had fallen.

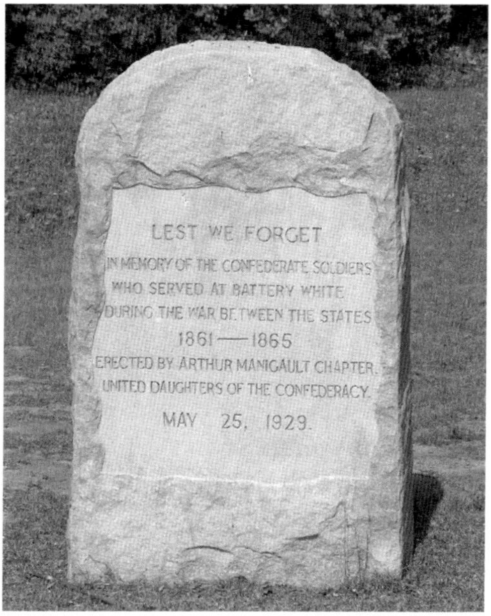

The United Daughters of the Confederacy monument marks the site of Battery White at Belle Isle. *Courtesy Scott Lawrence.*

Perhaps it was best that this needless effusion of blood never occurred, because by the time the battery was ready, the war was effectively, if not officially, over—and had been for some time. Yet Battery White stands as perhaps the one truly well-constructed fort built along what is now the Grand Strand, conceptualized, designed and built on a level with the best Confederate fortifications along the Atlantic coast.

Today, Battery White is the most complete and accessible of the many Civil War landmarks that can be found along the Grand Strand. While many of the original one hundred acres encompassing the trenches, stables and troops' quarters were long ago bulldozed and built over, a fairly significant portion of the water battery still exists. With nearly five hundred feet of earthworks remaining, the site is maintained as part of a condominium complex at the site of what was originally Belle Isle Plantation. Battery White was listed in the National Register on November 16, 1977, and so the remaining earthworks now appear to be safe from development. The earthworks are quite extensive, and one can see the remains of bombproofs, powder magazines and even a brick structure that predates the fort but was no doubt used by the Confederates as well. There is also a United Daughters of the Confederacy memorial marker at the site that was dedicated in 1929, as well as the two ten-inch Columbiads for which Trapier begged. They have been mounted on concrete and are truly impressive as they sit overlooking the bay, much as they did 150 years ago. In addition, three other cannons that were once at Battery White are still in the Georgetown area—two downtown in a waterside park on Front Street and one at the National Guard Armory at Highway 17 between Georgetown and McClellanville. Consequently, a ten- to fifteen-minute drive will allow visitors to see Battery White and five of the original sixteen guns found there in February 1865. It is a trip worth taking.

Chapter 5

Grand Strand Shipwrecks

Trying to write a comprehensive and completely accurate account of the hundreds of shipwrecks that exist along the coast from Georgetown to Little River is a nearly impossible task. Over the centuries, many area shipwrecks were simply logged as "Sunk near Georgetown, a brig" or in some similar way, with a date and perhaps a cargo. In other cases, passing ships noted wrecks as being washed up onshore (many such accounts were recorded in the vicinity of North Island), but the reporting ship was unable to identify the wreck. Frequent hurricanes in the area added to the toll, as well. Consequently, Lee Spence, in his work *Shipwrecks, Pirates & Privateers: Sunken Treasures of the Upper South Carolina Coast, 1521–1865*, notes more than three hundred area shipwrecks, and because the book in front of you is not *only* about shipwrecks, this chapter will only attempt to examine a few of the better-known, important and frequently documented shipwrecks in the area.

For the most part, shipwrecks along the strand seem to have occurred in clusters, becoming most numerous during the time of the Spanish privateers, the War of 1812, the Civil War and cataclysmic events such as hurricanes. For example, on September 4, 1834, a hurricane was responsible for the wrecks of the schooner *Maria*, the sloop *Exchange*, the schooner *John Stoney*, the brig *Francis Ann* and the schooner *Comet*, all in and around the Winyah Bay/Georgetown area. But what makes the fact that there are so many wrecks in the area so intriguing is that there are so few visible remains. Other than the boiler stack of the *Harvest Moon* in Winyah Bay and the (until recently) visible timbers of the *Freeda A. Wyley* (beach renourishment has probably only temporarily covered the wreck), there isn't much to see above water. In short, there are hundreds of wrecks in the area; though a number are accessible to divers, for the average person, reading about the wrecks is about as close as most of us are likely to come to them. Nevertheless, it is a fascinating look into the history of the area, and these shipwrecks provide a certain insight into the growth and development of the strand as a whole.

By far the area's most sought-after shipwreck is the first recorded wreck in the area and, in fact, the earliest documented in North America. Lucas Vazquez de Ayllon's flagship, the *Capitana*, was one of a fleet of a half-dozen ships headed for the vicinity of what is now Georgetown in order to establish a settlement in the New World. In 1526, de Ayllon's flagship grounded, probably near the entrance to Winyah Bay, and though the ship was laden with cargo and a total loss, all of the crew survived.

What makes the *Capitana* most noteworthy is that had a colony been established near Georgetown, as may have been intended before the loss of the ship and its supplies, that area, and not Charleston, would have been the first settled in the state; a large Spanish presence on the Carolina coast would have meant that the Grand Strand's history would have been quite different. Archaeologists continue to search for the ship, but Christopher Amer of the South Carolina Institute of Archaeology and Anthropology noted in an article in the *Coastal Observer* in 2008 that the search is difficult because the ship could even be *under* North or South Island. In 1526, South Island probably didn't even exist, and North Island would have been quite different indeed. Consequently, the mystery of the location of what is perhaps the area's most important shipwreck may never be known.

Sometimes ships simply wrecked even though no specific, continuous, overriding external factors (such as a war or storms) were the cause, as was the case of the *Anne and Sarah* and the *Hare*, both of which wrecked near Georgetown in 1744. But more often than not, there were systematic external causes, such as the Spanish pirates and privateers who plagued the area during the eighteenth century. They were especially busy in the area in 1762. In November, the privateer *St. Joseph* chased an English sloop ashore near the mouth of the Santee, and on December 5, a boatload of Spaniards rowed onto North Island, looted a house belonging to Mr. Dubourdieu and stole a boat. On December 10, the captured schooner *General Wolf*, which had been put into service as a Spanish privateer, chased another schooner ashore at North Island, and on December 13, the privateer *Sancta Maria* drove another schooner ashore near Georgetown.

During the Revolutionary War and the War of 1812, privateering once again became the cause of many wrecks, adding to the toll inflicted by the warships of the British and American navies. For example, a snow-brig was lost on the Georgetown Bar after being captured by the *Notre Dame* in May 1778, the brig *Peace and Harmony* was driven ashore in Winyah Bay by the American privateer *Vengeance* in March 1779 and the privateer *Peggy* chased ashore an unnamed sloop in Winyah Bay in July 1781. During the War of 1812, British warships were responsible for several wrecks. The prize brig *Tartar* was chased ashore at North Island in April 1813, and the schooner *Friends* was chased into Murrells Inlet and burned by the British in May 1814. American privateers took their toll, as well: a British schooner, probably the *Jasper*, may have been deliberately wrecked through sabotage on the Georgetown Bar in January 1814, and the captured British brig *Roper* was wrecked at Debordieu in November 1814.

Although it may seem that most wrecks occurred in Winyah Bay, there were many others up and down the coast. The schooner *Experiment* wrecked on what is probably now Litchfield Beach in 1806, the brig *Venus* foundered near Murrells Inlet in March 1809 and the schooner *Industry* stranded on the beach there that May. The brig *Matthew* wrecked in what is now Myrtle Beach in March 1812; the *Lucy Ann*, a schooner, wrecked in Murrells Inlet in January 1854; and the wreck of the one-hundred-foot-long *Horace Greeley* drifted ashore, bottom up and split open with both its stern and head missing, in October 1854. These are but a few of the wrecks noted in the area from the beginning of the nineteenth century until the period that would produce the greatest number of maritime casualties of all, the Civil War.

Early in the Civil War, several ships went down whose names are lost to us forever due to the inconsistent record keeping by the newly formed Confederate army. On August 9, 1861, a Union steamer sank after being wrecked by a storm off Georgetown, and the crew of nineteen was captured and placed in the Georgetown jail. On November 2, 1861, the steamer *Osceola*, commanded by Captain J.T. Morrill, foundered off Georgetown, and two boats of crewmen were taken captive.

The first really significant encounter involving a shipwreck and a battle, however, occurred on December 24, 1861, when the blockade runner *Prince of Wales* grounded while attempting to run in at North Inlet just above North Island. At about seven o'clock that morning, Union lieutenant Irvin Baxter of the USS *Gem of the Sea* saw the *Wales* running close to the shore and started firing at it. The third shot damaged the ship, and after four more shots the captain of the *Wales* had apparently had enough, and so he ran it into North Inlet. Just inside the bar, the ship grounded, and as the *Gem of the Sea* neared the beached runner, the runner's captain put the *Prince of Wales* to the torch

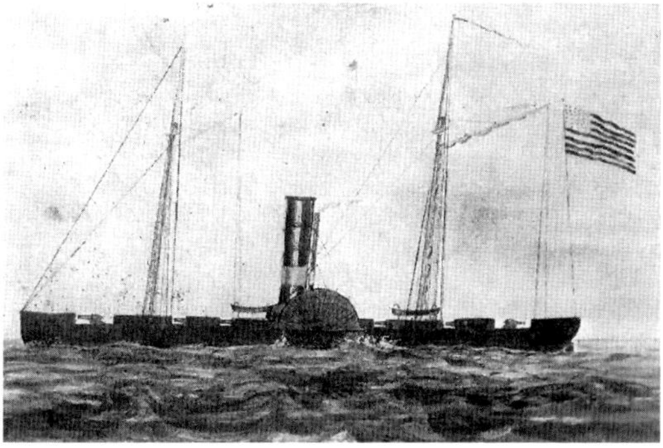

The USS *Sebago* unsuccessfully tried to tow off the supply ship *Lotus*, which wrecked on North Island. Even today, the wreck of the *Lotus* is sought for any remaining stores and artifacts it might hold. *Courtesy U.S. Navy Historical Center.*

before abandoning it. Union seamen from the *Gem of the Sea* tired to tow it off, but as they did so a company of Confederate cavalry opened fire on the Federals from the north shore of North Inlet, and under a heavy fire the ship ran aground once again. Baxter's men tried to tow the off ship yet again, but by that point they were also receiving fire from a separate Confederate patrol. Lieutenant Baxter later wrote that "the bullets fell over and around… as fast as the scoundrels could fire their pieces," and the Federals eventually gave up on trying to tow off the ship. Both sides watched the ship burn to the waterline, the Federals out a prize and the Confederates out a cargo of fruit and salt.

On April 10, 1862, the blockade runner *Liverpool* grounded trying to run into Georgetown, and its crew burned it to prevent its capture. A relatively rare event occurred on January 15, 1863, when a Union supply ship was wrecked on North Island. The *Lotus*, a ship out of Boston carrying supplies for the Federal troops stationed at Port Royal, ran ashore; though the Federals on the USS *Sebago* tried to tow it off, after moving it about twelve feet a storm surge pushed it even farther up the beach. The Federals decided that removing the ship was impracticable, and so began removing its cargo. Commander Beaumont of the *Sebago* noted that when his men were removing the cargo, they were surprised to find among the sutler's store and barrels of potatoes "casks of liquor…put up in various ways for smuggling." The Federals removed some of the cargo, though much had been lost when the ship beached.

On February 24, the English blockade runner *Queen of the Wave*, which Federal reports later called a "new and magnificent vessel," ran aground in the North Santee River, and it was set afire by its captain to keep it from being captured, even though its hold was full of valuable goods, including morphine, opium and quinine. But on the morning of the twenty-fifth, the

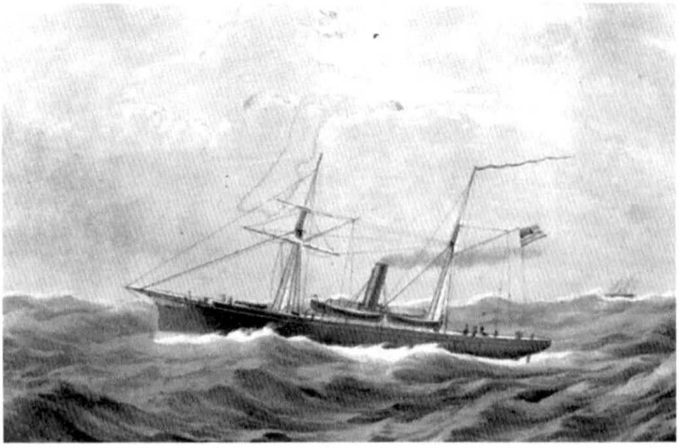

The USS *Monticello* was one of several Federal ships that shelled Murrells Inlet in an effort to stop the blockade running traffic there. *Courtesy U.S. Navy Historical Center.*

ship was still visible, and it was obvious that the fire had never reached the intensity needed to burn the ship and that the blaze had gone out. Lieutenant Commander T.H. Eastman of the USS *Conemaugh* immediately sent out boats to destroy the ship, lest the Confederates begin salvage operations and recover the ship's cargo. But as the *Conemaugh*'s men boarded the *Queen*, they discovered seven Confederate soldiers of the Waccamaw Light Artillery on board who had been conducting salvage operations all night. Unable to escape, the Confederates, led by Lieutenant Philip R. Lachicotte, were forced to surrender, were taken on board the Federal ship USS *Quaker City* and were ultimately sent to a northern prison. Eastmen's men completed the destruction of the ship by blowing up the *Queen of the Wave*.

The year 1863 would bring even more destruction to the shipping traffic along the strand. On April 27, the USS *Monticello* and the USS *Matthew Vassar* began shelling Murrells Inlet and, two hours later, landed more than fifty men to destroy as many ships and as much property in Murrells Inlet as they could. They first burned the schooner *Golden Liner* and then two houses, but as they turned to destroy another two schooners, a sloop and over two thousand bales of cotton, Confederate cavalry chased them back to their ships. The Federals would begin to pay greater attention to Murrells Inlet, however, after reports that the traffic there was "most brisk…averaging five to seven vessels a week." In October, the fifty-ton blockade runner *Rover*, loaded with cotton, attempted to run into Murrells Inlet on the seventeenth, and failing to do so, the schooner was driven ashore. Its crew removed the cargo to a spot behind the sand dunes and then put the ship to the torch, and two days later boats were sent out from the USS *T.A. Ward* under Ensign Myron Tillson to destroy the cargo and also the damaged schooner *Cecilia*, which was a mile and a half away. The *Ward*'s men were thwarted by Confederates from the Twenty-first Georgia Cavalry under Lieutenant Ely Kennedy, and Kennedy's men killed one of Tillson's men and captured several others, even though the Confederates faced a covering fire from both the barges and the *T.A. Ward*.

As 1864 began, there were several encounters with blockade runners seeking to enter Winyah Bay. The first of these involved the runner *Dare*, which had left Bermuda in early January; upon attempting to enter Wilmington, it had been chased off. It was pursued by the Federals until it was finally run aground twelve miles north of Georgetown at North Inlet on January 7. Rather than risk having the Federals tow it off, the captain of the runner evacuated the passengers and crew and set fire to the ship. Shortly thereafter, boats from the USS *Aries* and the USS *Montgomery* attempted to land a shore party of four officers and twenty-four sailors to put out the fire and salvage the ship, but halfway to shore the barges capsized in the rough seas and three of the Union seamen drowned. As the survivors from the barges made their way to shore, they found a party of three men—Major William P. White, commander of the Twenty-first Georgia Cavalry; Second Lieutenant Thomas Young; and Private Lemuel Robertson, both of Company C of White's regiment. The three Confederates, with no support and without firing a shot, "gallantly charged upon 25 Abolitionists…[and] armed with cutlasses and pistols…compell[ed] them to lay down their arms when there was no supporting forces within three quarters of a mile of the parties." Major White later explained that "to my surprise, instead of one volley at least, the whole party, commanded by a lieutenant of the U.S. Navy, obeyed the summons, were taken prisoners." Just a few days later, on January 12, the *Aries* would have more luck when it left the blockade runner *Vesta* "a complete wreck, with five feet of water in her" at Little River.

On June 2, 1864, a Union sentry in the North Island lighthouse spotted a ship lying close offshore near North Inlet at about nine o'clock that morning, and Master Charles W. Lee and the crew of the USS *Wamsutta* were informed soon thereafter. The ship was the side-wheel steamer *Rose*, and the *Wamsutta* would apparently chase it away from Winyah Bay. Owing to the low tide, the *Wamsutta* was unable to look for the ship any further until 3:00 p.m., but surprisingly, the *Rose* was still in the area. As soon as the *Rose* saw the *Wamsutta* approaching, it ran for the south end of Pawleys Island. Lee reported that it then "ran ashore near the wreck of another steamer and some buildings on the beach; the whole crew, consisting of about 20 persons, making their escape over the bows and by their boats, hastened by a rifle shell thrown at them by our 20-pounder Parrot."

The *Wamsutta* "threw a few shells and stands of grape into the buildings and woods and bushes, to clear them of any skulkers," and then Lee sent a boat's crew and specific orders to try and save the vessel if possible. Hardly had the Federals boarded it when a force of about seventy-five Confederate cavalrymen came from the direction of the north end of the island. Lee's men attempted to tow the *Wamsutta* off, but the runner was firmly grounded and immovable. By this time, "The cavalry had advanced to the edge of the woods, and commenced firing at our men on board the steamer, who returned their fire, and I also shelled the woods, which kept them back."

It was then nearly 7:00 p.m., and the Federals, finding it impossible to tow off the ship, decided to destroy its engines and then burn it to deny its contents to the Confederates. The only cargo the Federals discovered on board were "some barrels and cases of liquor and small stores," but Lee was certain that the ship had been unloaded during the afternoon as it sat at North Inlet. The *Wamsutta* remained offshore until the wreck was consumed by fire, and then it returned to its station near North Island. On June 9, Lee headed back to check the wreck and found "a large party of mounted men near the wreck and buildings, at which I fired several shells, stands of grape, and round shot." The bombardment drove away the Confederates, who "had apparently been at work trying to save the iron and parts of the machinery of the wreck of the *Rose*."

The destruction of the *Rose* was not significant in itself, for most of the cargo had ended up in Confederate hands as intended. But unbeknownst to the forces in the area at the time, the *Rose* would become perhaps the last blockade runner destroyed near Georgetown. After that, no Confederate ships would be successful trying to enter Winyah Bay because, as was the case in most Confederate ports in late 1864, the Union navy was now well in control of the surrounding waters. After the fall of Charleston on February 17, 1865, all major Southern ports were controlled by Federal forces, and Georgetown was one of the last large ports in Confederate hands. Within two months, the war would be over, but clearly the sparsely populated area between Georgetown and Little River had been a significant haven for blockade runners and a busy theatre for the Federal navy during the war as well.

Of course, after the Civil War, there were still plenty of wrecks, and one of these is without a doubt the Grand Strand's second most significant wreck (after the *Harvest Moon*): the *Freeda A. Wyley*. This wreck is well known largely because for almost one hundred years the remains of the burned-out wreck were visible in the sand at Forty-third Avenue North in Myrtle Beach. At one time, it had its own historical marker, it was featured on postcards and in brochures and it had the distinction of being one of the few remaining historical relics in Myrtle Beach, an area generally better known today for

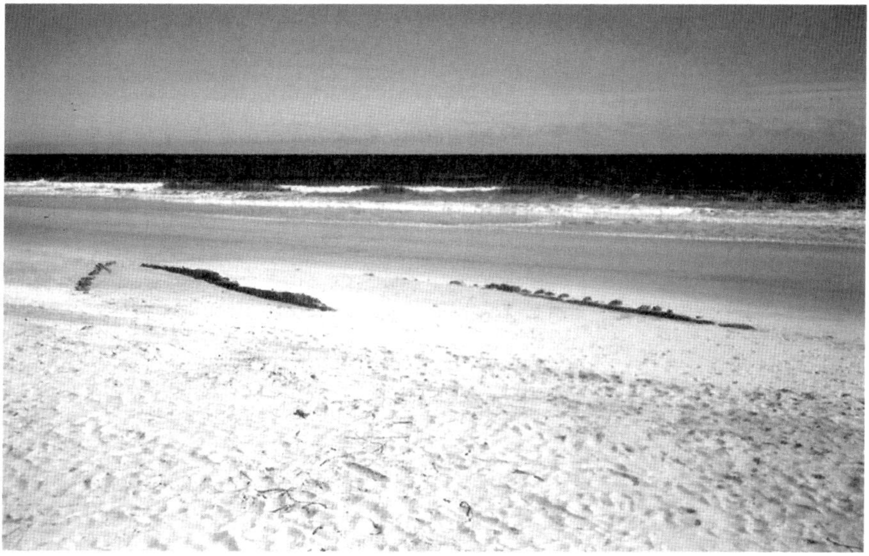

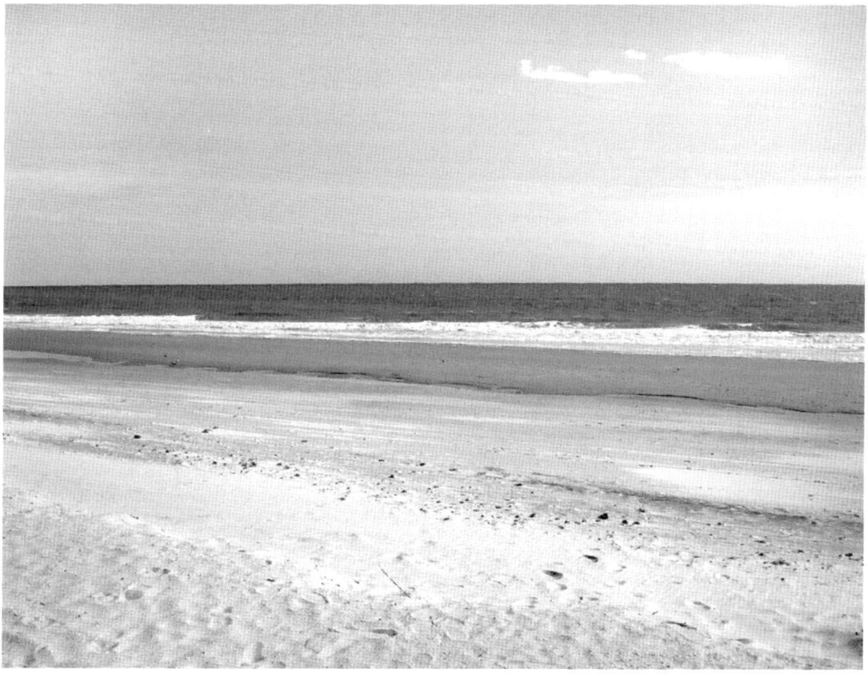

This page: The visible remains of the *Freeda A. Wyley* at Forty-third Avenue North in Myrtle Beach, photographed in 1988 by the author. The photograph of the same stretch of beach in 2010 illustrates how beach renourishment projects have now completely covered the wreck. *Photographs by the author.*

mini-golf, waterslides and amusement parks. Now, unfortunately, it has disappeared as surely as have the Ocean Forest Hotel, the German Prisoner of War Camp and the blockhouse at Fort Randall.

Like many local shipwrecks, the *Freeda A. Wyley* was the victim of a hurricane, the Great Storm of 1893. During the storm, nearly one hundred ships were lost, more than two thousand people died and another thirty thousand people were left homeless. A three-masted, 507-ton barkentine carrying a load of yellow pine from Thomaston, Maine, to Pascagoula, Mississippi, the *Freeda A. Wyley* found itself caught in the high winds and treacherous seas as the storm reached its peak on August 29, 1893. Though no witnesses lived to explain exactly what happened to the ship, it was last seen by the schooner *Yamasee* burning off Frying Pan Shoals near Cape Fear during the height of the storm. Though the *Yamasee* searched, it found no survivors, and only the captain's log, whose last entry reportedly noted, "Heaven help us," was later recovered near Shalotte, North Carolina. The hulk, burned to the waterline, later drifted ashore at what is now Forty-third Avenue in Myrtle Beach.

For many years, the wreck of the *Freeda A. Wyley* was visible on and off throughout the year, especially in the winter. In the 1990s, beach renourishment projects designed to rebuild the devastated beaches ravaged by hurricanes such as Hurricane Hugo necessitated covering the remains of the wreck with sand. Given the way area beaches are constantly changing, however, few locals residents would be willing to bet that the wreck won't eventually surface once again.

Another ship lost in 1893 was the *Jonathan May*, and like the *Freeda A. Wyley* it came ashore in Myrtle Beach—in this case at what is now Seventy-fifth Avenue North. A slightly smaller three-masted schooner than the *Freeda* at 379 tons, the *Jonathan May* also carried timber and was sailing out of Philadelphia when it, too, strayed into the path of a hurricane. It capsized near Frying Pan Shoals, though the crew's ending was happier than that of the *Freeda A. Wyley.* The *May*'s crew was found clinging to wreckage, was rescued by the schooner *Ann E. Valentine* and was returned home. The ship didn't fare so well. When it drifted ashore near Singleton's Swash in what is now Myrtle Beach, it was stripped of its cargo of lumber, and everything usable was hauled away from the wreck by locals, who came from miles around for the building supplies the wreck provided. For many years, the *May* was visible, as was the *Freeda A. Wyley*, but after Hurricane Hazel in 1954, the wreck was apparently shattered and strewn throughout the sand and water. For years, bits and pieces would reportedly surface, though Hurricane Hugo

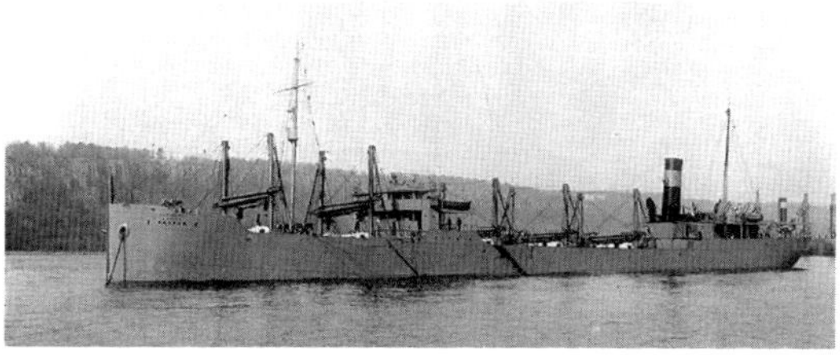

The USS *Hector* went down off Georgetown in 1916. *Courtesy U.S. Navy Historical Center.*

apparently smashed and buried the ship once and for all. Perhaps, however, another storm will one day expose what's left of the *Jonathan May*'s wreckage once again.

In 1916, one of the first notable wrecks of the twentieth century occurred when the USS *Hector* went down off Georgetown. An 11,230-ton naval collier, the *Hector* was commissioned in 1909. It was used to transport coal for the Atlantic fleet and also naval goods and supplies from the United States to the Philippines. It was wrecked on July 14, 1916.

The SS *Hebe* and the HMS *St. Cathan* wrecks, often referred to as the "Twin Cities," can be found off Murrells Inlet. During World War II, the British ship *St. Cathan* was a subchaser and convoy escort, but it found neither submarine nor cargo when it was rammed in the starboard quarter by the Dutch freighter *Hebe* one night in 1942 when both were apparently running without lights to avoid the German U-boats in abundance along the North and South Carolina coasts. The *Hebe* went down in about a half-hour, but its entire crew was rescued. The crew of the *St. Cathan* was not so lucky—the ship went down in less than five minutes, and of its thirty-nine crewmen just nine were rescued. Today, the *Hebe* lies on its port side, and the *St. Cathan* sits about a fourth of a mile away roughly one hundred feet below the surface.

While modern technology no doubt has prevented many shipwrecks, in rare instances cases it can also cause them. A case in point was when, on January 23, 1953, the schooner *Fiddler's Green* was wrecked when a flashlight positioned near its magnetic compass caused a deviation error, and so its trip from Baltimore to Trinidad met an untimely end on Pawleys Island.

Nevertheless, just as was true centuries ago, nature is responsible for most wrecks in the area, and such was the case with the *City of Richmond*, the 294-foot steel-hulled ship that had been a ferry and was on its way from Virginia to the Virgin Islands to be converted to an upscale casino ship. Period pictures show that while its outside may have looked a little weatherworn from years of service, the interior of the ship certainly lent itself to refurbishing and upgrading to a luxury vessel. Polished wood interiors, broad staircases and

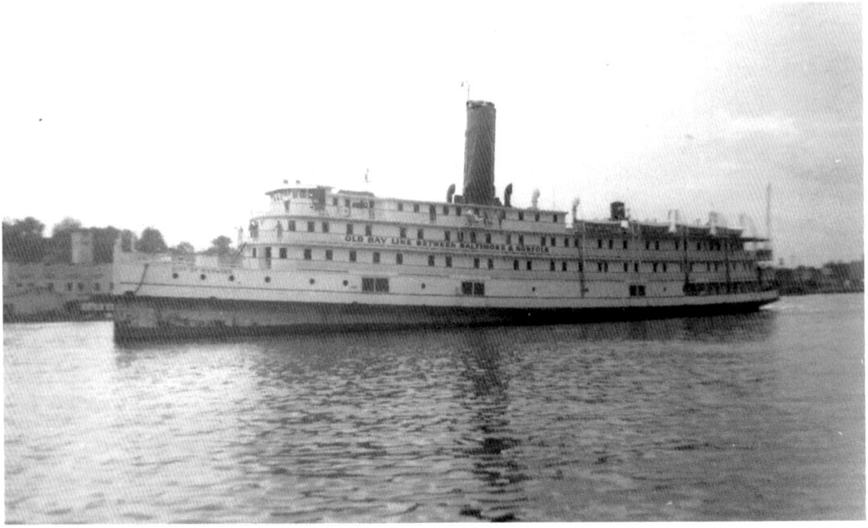

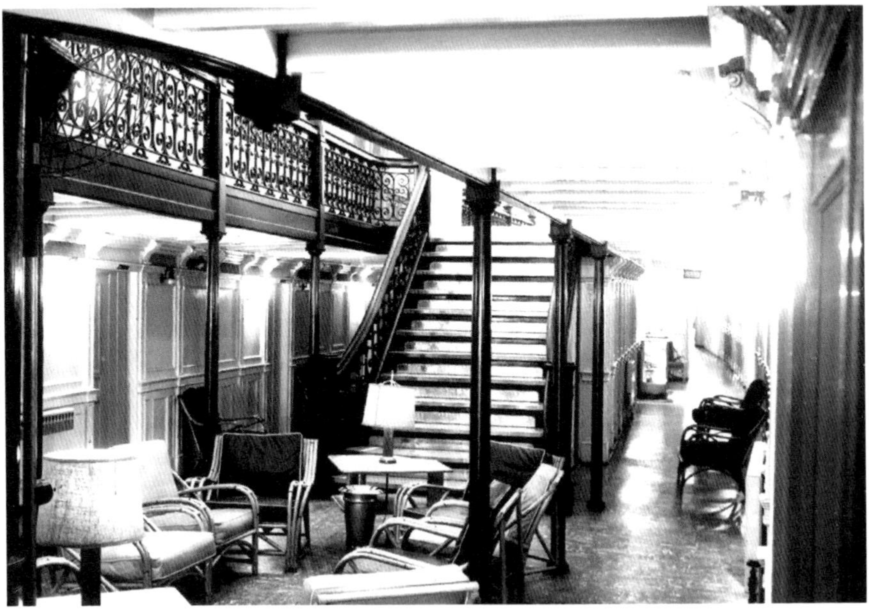

This and next page: The *City of Richmond*, with its lush interior and spacious five-deck layout, was slated to serve out its days as a casino ship in the Virgin Islands before it met an untimely demise off Georgetown. As these pictures of the after lounge and main staircase show, its interior was well suited for that purpose. *Courtesy Jack Shaum/the Steamship Historical Society of America.*

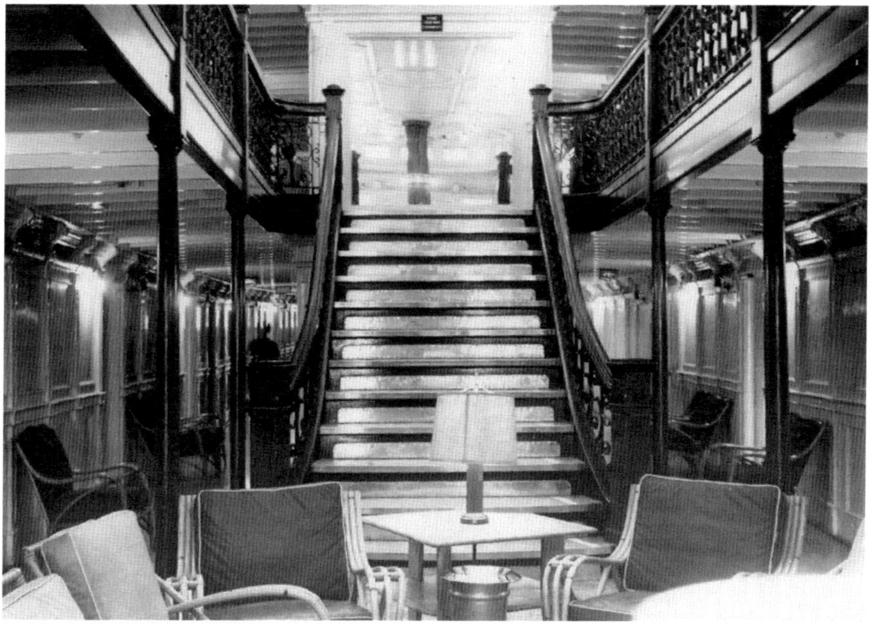

an abundance of deck access areas show why the *City of Richmond* was a good choice for conversion. It was never to be, however, because while about fifteen miles off Georgetown, it sank in about fifty feet of water in October 1961. Because the five-deck vessel was so large, at that depth its smokestack and superstructure were a navigational peril and had to be blown off the wreck. Though the ship is otherwise largely intact, it is collapsed at the stern. This doesn't deter divers, and today the *City of Richmond* is one of the area's most popular wrecks.

Even today, with all man's ability to prevent wrecks, they continue to occur, though no doubt less frequently than in the past. In 1996, the schooner *Frolic* wrecked at North Jetty entering Winyah Bay, and as recently as 2007 and 2008, both a seventy-foot yacht and a forty-six-foot catamaran wrecked on North Jetty as well. For all the wrecks in the area, however, other than the USS *Harvest Moon*, none is currently visible above water, although many rest just below the shallow waters off the coast or below the shifting sands of area beaches waiting to be revealed. Clearly, shipwrecks have been, and will always be, a lasting legacy along the Grand Strand.

Chapter 6

The Legend of the Grand Strand U-boats

While today most people know the Grand Strand as one of the most important centers of tourism in the United States, there is a significance related to the area's measurable history and its relationship to the sea that is much deeper and, some would say, much more impressive. The Spanish, French and English all had ships visit this area while exploring the New World, and in fact some of the earliest accounts of this area come from these explorers. Privateers and pirates frequented this coast; British warships and American ships hunted one another here during both the Revolutionary War and the War of 1812; and during the Civil War, Federal and Confederate warships and blockade runners played a cat-and-mouse game in every cove and inlet from the South Santee to Little River. Since the twentieth century, however, one might argue that history has given way to tourism and that little of any real international historical significance occurred here from the late nineteenth century on. Oddly enough, it was during the twentieth century that the most enigmatic events relating to this area's history occurred (or didn't occur, depending on your perspective)—that being when German U-boats supposedly visited the Grand Strand.

If one were to go on the hints and allegations of the press from the 1940s, as well as the rumors and myths that have grown to near legendary proportions since that time, then U-boats most certainly did roam the Grand Strand during World War II. Frankly, the idea isn't all that far-fetched, and one need only look to our neighbors to the north for evidence that it could have happened.

Because North Carolina's Outer Banks extend far into the Atlantic, shipping lanes often take ships quite near the shores there; as a result,

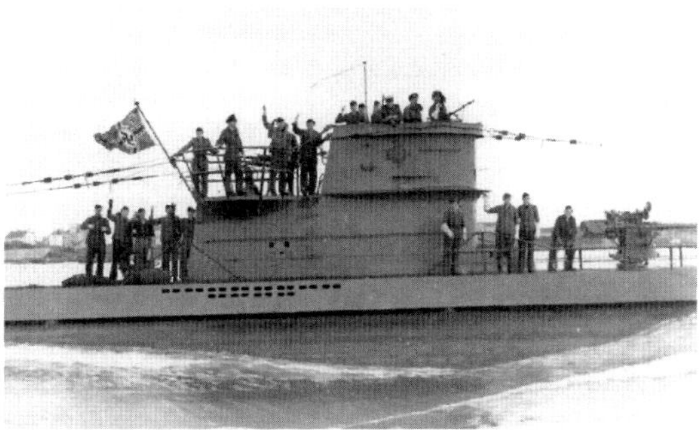

A wartime picture of the conning tower of the German submarine *U-203*. *Courtesy U.S. Navy Historical Center.*

during World War II the area already known as the "Graveyard of the Atlantic" earned another nickname—"Torpedo Alley"—as it became a shooting gallery for U-boats that would lie in wait off the coast and torpedo unsuspecting ships carrying supplies badly needed for the Allied war effort. At least four hundred ships were torpedoed, and more than five thousand sailors lost their lives off the Outer Banks during World War II; in fact, five ships went down in one night alone in 1942. The U-boats themselves were not immune from destruction however, and the price they paid for the devastation they inflicted on shipping along the North Carolina coast was that their own losses included the *U-85*, the *U-352*, the *U-521*, the *U-548*, the *U-576* and the *U-701*, all of which lie off the North Carolina and lower Virginia coasts today.

Consequently, it is obvious that German U-boats were at least in proximity to the South Carolina coast during World War II; even if the shipping lanes weren't as close to our coast as they were in North Carolina, no doubt an occasional U-boat passed by the stretch of coast from Georgetown to Little River, and they probably trained their periscopes on it from time to time. However, there were no known allied ships torpedoed in the Grand Strand area and no confirmed sightings of U-boats in this region at all. Nevertheless, anyone who grew up along the strand probably remembers hearing that U-boats visited this coast during the war, and one seldom meets a longtime resident of the strand who *hasn't* heard these rumors. But with no physical evidence of any type, nor confirmed sightings, where did these very prevalent rumors about U-boats frequenting this region originate—or, indeed, the even more intriguing rumors regarding U-boats working with the assistance of collaborators in the area?

Answering this question is fairly complicated, as the convergence and separation of what is history and legend can often be. The first place to

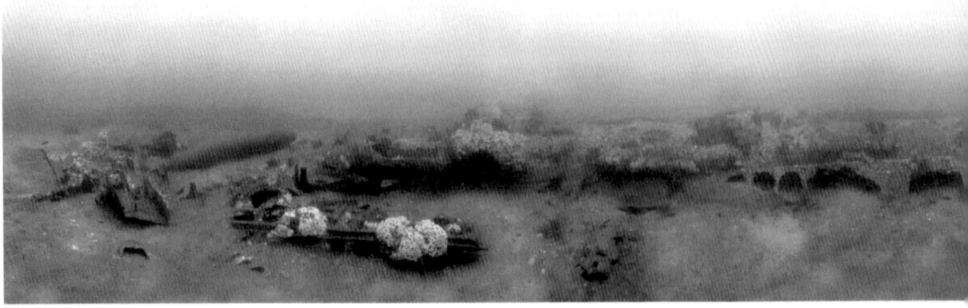

It is obvious from this modern-day picture of the wreck of the *U-85*, seen here as it lies underwater off the North Carolina coast, that German U-boats did indeed prowl local waters during World War II. *Courtesy NOAA's Office of National Marine Sanctuaries.*

turn to for documentation of accounts of U-boats visiting the area is the area press during the war, and in this case the local newspaper known as the *Horry Herald* provided ample fuel to stoke fears that residents may have had about German invaders reaching these shores. Area residents were no doubt aware of the possibility of submarines lurking in local waters, though perhaps attempts to alert local residents to the dangers facing them may have induced an almost unreasonable panic.

On June 25, 1942, the *Horry Herald* instructed residents "to give a wide berth to any torpedoes, mines, aerial bombs, depth charges, or other objects suspected of being explosive, which may wash up on the beach" and that some "are so sensitive that the mere footsteps of a person approaching too close may set them off." On February 18, 1943, an article reported a mysterious unidentified body in an advanced state of decomposition that washed up

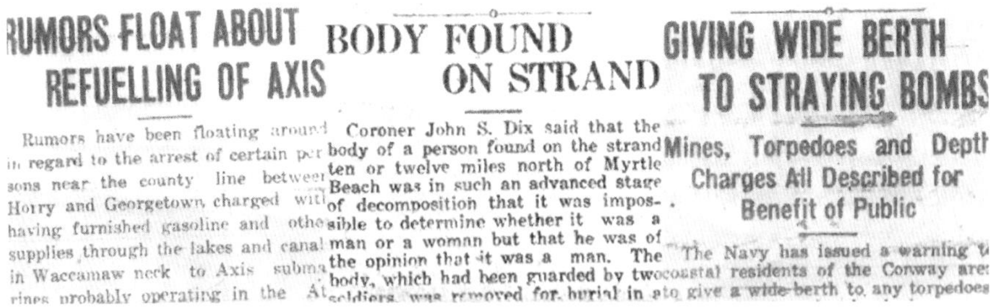

RUMORS FLOAT ABOUT REFUELLING OF AXIS

Rumors have been floating around in regard to the arrest of certain persons near the county line between Horry and Georgetown charged with having furnished gasoline and other supplies through the lakes and canal in Waccamaw neck to Axis submarines probably operating in the At

BODY FOUND ON STRAND

Coroner John S. Dix said that the body of a person found on the strand ten or twelve miles north of Myrtle Beach was in such an advanced stage of decomposition that it was impossible to determine whether it was a man or a woman but that he was of the opinion that it was a man. The body, which had been guarded by two soldiers was removed for burial in

GIVING WIDE BERTH TO STRAYING BOMBS

Mines, Torpedoes and Depth Charges All Described for Benefit of Public

The Navy has issued a warning to coastal residents of the Conway area to give a wide berth to any torpedoes

Lurid headlines such as these from Horry County papers no doubt added to locals' fears that German U-boats were patrolling our beaches and, worse, that collaborators were in their midst.

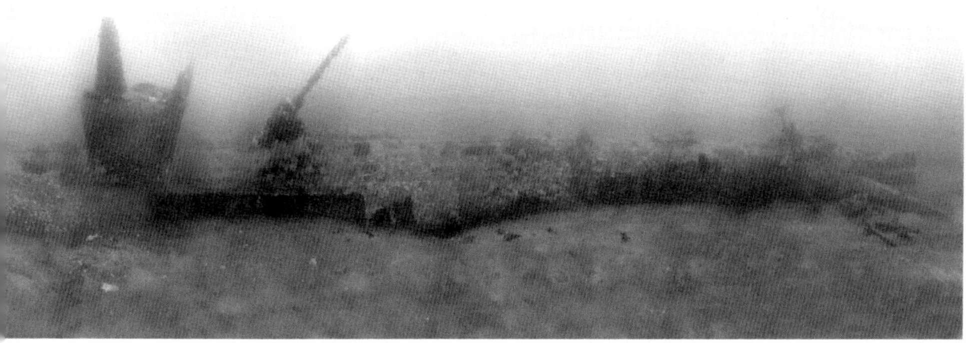

north of Myrtle Beach, "which had been guarded by two soldiers," giving the impression—correctly or not—that the corpse was militarily related. Newsworthy items such as these coupled with front-page headlines about heavy shipping losses along the eastern seaboard no doubt led area residents to suspect that German U-boats lurked menacingly just off the coast.

If U-boats were right off our coast, didn't Winyah Bay and the access to the North and South Santee, Sampit, Waccamaw and Black Rivers present inviting opportunities as well? One such rumor that many people have heard is that during the war U-boats entered the Intracoastal Waterway via Winyah Bay. In theory, this would seem to have been a good tactical maneuver for the Germans. The waterway was completed in the late 1930s, and during the war many supplies were shipped on barges via the waterway because it provided safer passage than did the ocean. But though the concept of a German U-boat entering the waterway might have sounded good in theory, putting it into practice would have been another matter altogether.

In many places the waterway is only 12 feet deep, but this doesn't seem to deter many people from accepting the idea that a submarine could cruise, submerged and undetected, through those shallow waters. And while it might have been possible for a surfaced U-boat to have entered the Intracoastal Waterway, once in the waterway, maneuverability would have been almost impossible. The average width of the waterway is 90 feet, while the length of a standard World War II U-boat was 220 feet, its beam (width) averaged 21 feet and its draught (height) averaged 15 feet. As a result, at most places in the waterway, a submarine would have not been maneuverable and would have been essentially trapped. Although it is possible that at some time a U-boat commander may have deliberated entering the waterway, it is doubtful that any officer worthy of rank would have placed his ship and crew so clearly in harm's way. Because the channel was shallow, the U-boats in the waterway would have had to run on the surface, and since, as will be discussed later, there were Army Air Corps planes stationed at Myrtle Beach, that wasn't likely to have happened. Consequently, it is highly doubtful and almost absurd to think that U-boats cruised the Intracoastal Waterway along the South Carolina coast.

As implausible as the idea that U-boats entered the waterway may be, there are other rumors that are even greater strains on credibility. The first time I ever researched this subject (in the late 1980s), a local librarian discovered the topic that I was writing about and asked, "Have you ever heard that the Huntingtons had something to do with the German submarines in this area during World War II? People come in and ask about it all the time, but we never know what to tell them." The "Huntingtons" were Archer Milton and Anna Hyatt Huntington, and during World War II, they were the owners of the property that encompasses the area known as Brookgreen Gardens and Huntington Beach State Park today. Even seventy years later, it does seem to be the question that won't go away, and in an interview with Robin Salmon at Brookgreen Gardens in 2009, she informed me that the question *still* frequently comes up when people visit the gardens. Truly, perhaps no speculation involving the enigma of the U-boats has received as much attention as the question of whether the Huntingtons were collaborating with the Germans during the World War II. Several different rumors involving the Huntingtons have circulated, and in the interest of dispelling the U-boat myths once and for all, they must be addressed.

Archer Milton and Anna Hyatt Huntington purchased over six thousand acres south of Murrells Inlet in 1930. The Huntingtons were extremely wealthy, and within a short time they had acquired more than nine thousand acres encompassing all of what is now known as Brookgreen Gardens and Huntington Beach State Park. They were interested in building a winter home here, so in 1931 they began work on the magnificent structure now known as Atalaya.

The construction of Atalaya provided jobs for many local people at a time when jobs were badly needed. Most of the major construction was completed in 1932, and for nearly a decade the Huntingtons stayed at Atalaya during the milder South Carolina winters and then returned north during the summer. Most local residents, however, probably felt that they had almost nothing in common with the Huntingtons. The Huntingtons possessed great wealth during the Depression, a time when many people could hardly afford to eat, and they were well educated and had traveled extensively; during the 1930s and '40s, before the local real estate and tourism boom, many

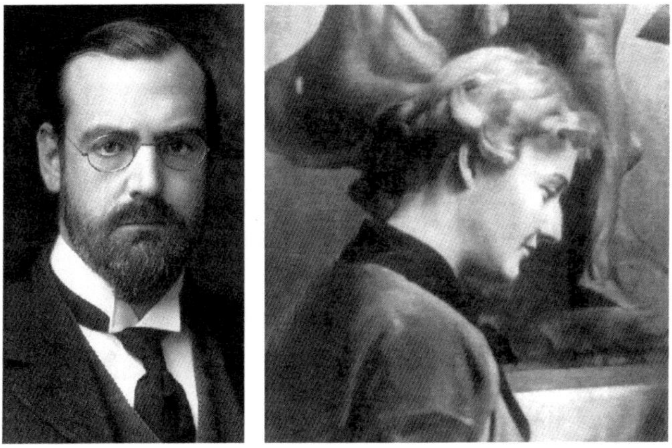

This page: Because Anna Hyatt and Archer Milton Huntington were wealthy and from the North, some locals may have distrusted them, which may have also led to suspicions that they were German collaborators.

rural Georgetown and Horry County residents were poorly educated and many had probably not traveled as far as the state capital. No doubt many local people wondered why the Huntingtons would want to live in such an isolated place with no close neighbors, and to some people this in itself may have been cause for gossip. Irrational though it may seem today, from the start the Huntingtons were branded as being outsiders (and Yankees at that), and as is often the case, outsiders were considered untrustworthy.

Though it is not exactly clear where the idea of the Huntingtons as German collaborators may have originated, as had been the case with feeding the fears of the public in relation to U-boats visiting these shores, the press may have been responsible for connecting the imaginary dots linking the Huntingtons to the rumors of collaborators. Shortly after the United States entered the war, the July 25, 1942 edition of the *Horry Herald* printed the following item on the front page:

> *RUMORS FLOAT ABOUT REFUELLING OF AXIS*
> *Rumors have been floating around in regard to the arrest of certain persons near the county line between Horry and Georgetown charged with having furnished gasoline and other supplies through the lakes and canals in the Waccamaw Neck to Axis submarines probably operating in the Atlantic Ocean…Other stories were that strange boats had been washed up on the shore, boats not manufactured in this country, and their ownership unknown. There are still other stories which cannot be believed because none have been reported to the newspaper and we cannot find any person who has personal knowledge of the matter.*

In an area where so many people were already fearful of the proximity of German submarines (during the six months prior to the appearance of the *Horry Herald*'s article, almost sixty Allied ships and two U-boats were sunk off the coast of North Carolina), this article no doubt sparked countless rumors as to the identity of the collaborators. Perhaps to some it almost stood to reason that since the Huntingtons lived in the area mentioned in the newspaper, and because they were so much different from the other local residents, they must have known something about the U-boats. Whether this article was the origin of the Huntington rumors is unknown, but more and more questions arose over time, fueling more graphic rumors about the Huntingtons as collaborators. Some of the rumors that have emerged in the intervening years since the war are so interesting—if far-fetched—that they deserve some comment.

A U-BOAT TUNNEL RUNS UNDERNEATH ATALAYA AND BROOKGREEN

For many years, there has been a rumor that a tunnel to the Waccamaw River runs underneath Atalaya and Brookgreen and that through this tunnel subs entered the waterway to refuel before patrolling the coast. Though to some people this idea may seem preposterous, interestingly enough it is one of the most widespread of the rumors involving German submarines being in the area during World War II. The inspiration for this tale seems to come from the fact that when the Huntingtons bought and then developed parts

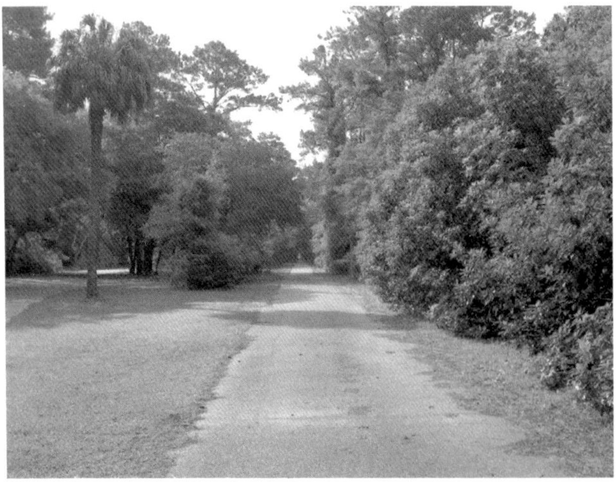

Some people believed that a tunnel ran underneath this road (in what is now Huntington Beach State Park) from the ocean to the Waccamaw River and that, through it, U-boats accessed U-boat pens maintained by the Huntingtons. *Photograph by the author.*

of the Brookgreen property, they built a straight concrete road from Atalaya to Brookgreen, and it is underneath this road that the tunnel supposedly existed. However, this rumor simply defies logic. If one were simply to follow the road line and build a tunnel straight from the beach to the Waccamaw River, it would be more than three miles long, the tunnel would have to extend well out into the ocean—to where the water was deep enough to give the subs access—and the tunnel would have to be at least twenty to twenty-five feet deep and wide as well. Considering that the road was built a decade before the war by local workers, wouldn't it seem that if an engineering project of the magnitude of a massive subterranean tunnel had taken place at least one person could verify this story?

U-BOATS OFF THE COAST WERE REFUELED WITH AID FROM THE SHORE

Many people believed that, using the lights of Atalaya as a guide, the U-boats waited off the coast at night while they were refueled with aid from the shore. This rumor was probably given credence because many residents of Murrells Inlet and the surrounding area could recall seeing lights offshore at night during the war. Actually, this doesn't prove a thing, since many ships did not observe blackout rules, and light flashes over the ocean at night could even have been U-boat attacks and explosions taking place far away from these shores. Therefore, although lights may well have been seen offshore at night, there is no foundation for the belief that they were U-boats being refueled by anyone, much less the Huntingtons. Similar rumors claim that captured U-boats had American groceries in their larders, because German sailors went ashore at night and bought them. These stories are simply rumors and seem to have no foundation in fact at all.

U-BOAT PENS WERE BUILT BEHIND BROOKGREEN

According to this legend, the U-boats would enter Winyah Bay below Georgetown and then head upriver until they entered a private canal owned by the Huntingtons. Once there, they found refueling docks made of reinforced concrete, where they could tie up and pass the time safely. Then the refueled the subs would either head on up the waterway or back out through Winyah Bay and into the ocean. A Georgetown man told me that as a child he had actually seen these pens. When I asked him their location, he told me that a U.S. Navy demolition team had blown them up in the 1960s, as they were somewhat of an embarrassment.

Actually, there is a basis for this story, but one that has nothing to do with U-boats. According to Robin Salmon, vice-president for Collections and Curator of Sculpture at Brookgreen Gardens, there were structures behind Brookgreen on the river, but they were "a late-nineteenth century barge canal, landing, and dock that were expanded in the early twentieth century at Laurel Hill Plantation, the northernmost part of Brookgreen Gardens' property." At one time, Brookgreen had an extensive complex of works to facilitate the production and milling of rice, and the dock and landing were there for that reason. True, when the Huntingtons built a home at Laurel Hill in the 1930s (Anna Huntington's physician apparently felt it would be better for her health not to live at Atalaya, and as such directly on the ocean, in the winter), Archer Huntington had the docks rebuilt—just as would anyone who lived on a lake or a river. According to Salmon, in the 1960s "the president of Brookgreen Gardens destroyed what was left of the newer dock in order to keep trespassers and poachers from using it to enter the property from the river." In addition, there is another dock behind Brookgreen that was built in the 1930s, which today is an observation platform "for birdwatchers and others interested in viewing wildlife." In short, there were and are docks, but no U-boat pens, and nothing beyond the run-of-the-mill landings and piers anyone who owned a home on a lake or river might build.

There Is a Sunken German Submarine off Huntington Beach

The first time I heard this was from a local educator, who claimed that the U.S. Navy sunk the submarine with depth charges. He said that he had heard that not only was the sub there, but that it was also the site of a great deal of relic hunting by scuba divers. While there are a number of popular U-boat dive sites along the North Carolina coast, all it takes is a call to any one of the local dive shops to know that there is no sunken U-boat in our area. If the sub were there, it would no doubt be a landmark.

THE U.S. NAVY CAPTURED A GERMAN SUBMARINE OFF HUNTINGTON BEACH

The story behind this is that the navy caught the submarine intact while the Germans were on the surface refueling. According to rumor, many of the German sailors were even found to have ticket stubs in their pockets, supposedly from local theatres. Unfortunately for those who would like to believe this story, during World War II only five German U-boats—the *U-505*, *U-110*, *U-570*, *U-744* and *U-1024*—were captured intact, and several of those sunk while being taken into port. All were captured far away from these shores (the *U-505* west of Africa, the *U-110* and *U-570* near Iceland, the *U-744* in the North Atlantic and the *U-1024* in the Irish Sea), so there is obviously no credence to this rumor, either.

Many of these somewhat preposterous myths seem to be based on the supposition that the Huntingtons sat out the war in Brookgreen and that the isolated location gave them the opportunity to assist the Germans unbeknownst to the locals. However, there are several very important facts that some of these rumors seem to ignore. First, during World War II, the Huntingtons did not live at Atalaya. They moved north to Connecticut for

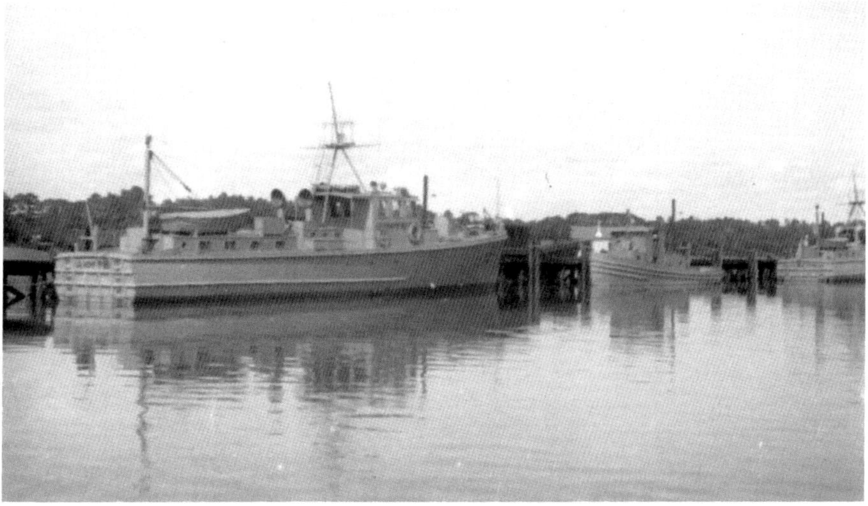

In addition to the airfield in Myrtle Beach, the presence of the army crash boat base in Murrells Inlet, seen here in 1944, would have made it unlikely that U-boats would have found the Waccamaw Neck area an appealing base of operations. *Courtesy Murrells Inlet 2020 and the Georgetown County Digital Library.*

the duration of the war, and ironically, during 1943 and 1944, their home at Brookgreen was occupied by the U.S. Air Corps. A radar unit was installed, a temporary airfield was set up, Atalaya was fortified with machine guns and the more than five hundred men serving there patrolled the beaches and assisted the 455th Bomber Squadron stationed in Myrtle Beach. Even the riverside property was used, as the house on the property at Laurel Hill was turned into a mess hall. Secondly, in Murrells Inlet, which is just a few hundred yards from the Huntington property, the military had a crash boat group on station during the war. These units frequently patrolled the waters, and consequently, between the air corps using the area for training and gunnery exercises and the crash boats patrolling the area waters, and it seems foolish to think that German U-boats could have operated with impunity right under their noses.

In many cases, colorful folklore tends to add a certain ambiance to an area. Unfortunately, in some cases, legend becomes accepted as fact, often making it necessary to dig deeper than the legend and see if there is any substance to the rumors. While it is possible that U-boats may have occasionally visited the waters offshore of the Grand Strand, it is doubtful that they ever entered the Intracoastal Waterway, were assisted by local collaborators or in fact did much more than view our shores from afar with the aid of a periscope.

Chapter 7

The Hot and Hot Fish Club, and the Hidden History of Drunken Jack Island

The history of the Hot and Hot Fish Club epitomizes the Old South and the opulence and grandeur of antebellum lifestyles, and the legend of Drunken Jack Island recalls the bloodthirsty pirates who once roamed the Carolina coast in search of plunder. Oddly enough, these two are linked together, a mixture of both fact and fiction connected by a drunken Revolutionary War soldier and the island that he called his home. Add a long-lost Confederate fort to the mix, and you have the hidden and confounding history of a now deserted island in Murrells Inlet that is the basis of a tale for the ages.

Before the Civil War, the area between Georgetown and Murrells Inlet was home to a number of the nation's richest landowners, many of whom were important locally and nationally. These local land barons raised rice and indigo and owned and sometimes managed immense estates worked by thousands of slaves. Like the wealthy today, they had a need for conviviality and socialization, yet unlike their modern-day counterparts, jetting to some far-off, exotic locale was obviously out of the question. At a time when travel might take months, and in an age before the existence of the ubiquitous country clubs of today, the wealthy had to come up with their own localized diversions. One of the first and most famous of these in the Grand Strand area was the Hot and Hot Fish Club of All Saints Parish, an organization whose origins and exclusive membership date back to before the War of 1812.

The Hot and Hot Fish Club's earliest meetings seem to have been get-togethers for a few local influential planters and patriots to drink, eat and

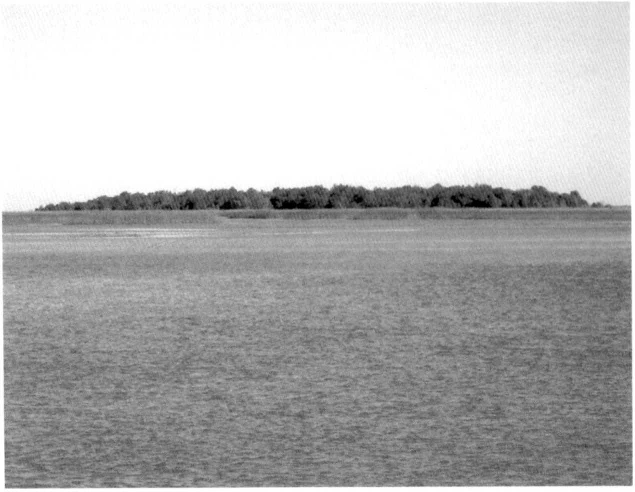

Drunken Jack Island in Murrells Inlet was the first home of the Hot and Hot Fish Club. *Photograph by the author.*

discuss events and problems of the times. Robert F.W. Allston, who would himself become a member as an adult and who would also serve as governor of South Carolina from 1856 to 1858, remembered that even as a boy of fifteen in 1816, the club was a well-established part of the planter's lives. When Allston was a boy, the clubhouse was located on what would be the first of five locations, the island now known as Drunken Jack Island in Murrells Inlet.

The procedure on meeting days was simple: the men would fish until a predetermined time and then they would take their catch to the clubhouse to be prepared by their servants. The fish would be prepared and then served with a number of other epicurean delights, such as beef, ham, fresh game and rice. To these main courses would be added the extras that members were responsible for providing, including bread, vegetables and anything else they desired to add to the feast. The courses were served in succession, with one type of food being served hot right after another, hence the name "Hot and Hot." Washed down with the finest wines and spirits that their cellars could provide, their feasts were legendary, on a par with the feudal lords of old Europe. The club's membership in these early days included Jack Green, John H. Tucker, Major J. Ward, Francis Marion Weston, Benjamin Allston, Robert Withers, William Tucker, F. Burrington Thomas, Major W.A. Bull, Davison McDowell, General Joseph Waties Aliston, John G. North, Captain Thomas Petigru (USN), Thomas Howe, John Hays Allston and Dr. W.A. Norris. Many of these names will be familiar to local historians, as they were in a sense the founding fathers of many aspects of life in the Georgetown/Waccamaw Neck region of the coast.

From their organization's simple and relatively informal origins grew a more formalized agenda of "convivial and social intercourse" as the club's affluent membership grew, and a more expansive range of activities and diversions was offered as well. After the original clubhouse was damaged by a hurricane, it was rebuilt on the mainland at Murrells Inlet. As the membership grew, the clubhouse changed locations several times, ultimately ending up at Pawleys Island. The clubhouse built there was on a ten-acre grant of land owned by Colonel T. Pinckney Alston, and this last clubhouse included a large kitchen with chimney, a meeting room, a tenpin alley and billiard table.

With the erection of this new and rather lavish clubhouse, by 1845 the membership had grown to the point where members developed a set of rules to govern themselves, though leadership was hardly a problem for the membership that included two governors (Joseph Alston and R.F.W Allston) and two lieutenant governors (Joshua Ward and Plowden C.J. Weston), as well as a number of prominent local planters, doctors and lawyers. In addition, many members had served in the military (their ranks including one general, eleven colonels, two majors and two captains) in Revolutionary War, the War of 1812 and the Mexican War, and with the coming of the Civil War, many of the members would find themselves officers in the state militia and eventually in the Confederate army. The membership during the mid-nineteenth century included Dr. John D. Magill, Dr. Edward Thomas Heriot, Colonel F. W. Heriot, Francis Weston, Colonel Joshua John Ward, W. Percival Vaux, R.F.W. Allston, Colonel P.W. Fraser, Dr. Andrew Hasell, Hugh Fraser, Joshua W. LaBruce, John LaBruce, Robert Nesbit, Colonel T. Pinckney Alston, Colonel J. Motte Alston, Dr. B. Burgh Smith, Colonel John Ashe Alston, Colonel J. Harleston Read Jr., Joshua Ward, Colonel Charles Alston Jr., Dr. John H. Tucker, William Hyrne Tucker, Plowden C.J. Weston, Dr. William Magill, Joseph Magill, Dr. Arthur B. Flagg, Dr. Allard B. Flagg, Nathaniel Barnwell, Joseph Alston Jr., Dr. E. Belin Flagg, Robert H. Nesbit, William Allan Allston, Dr. William M. Post, Colonel J. Blythe Allston, Captain Mayham Ward, Colonel D.W. Jordan, Dr. Henry M. Tucker and Colonel Benjamin Allston. Clearly this was a club only for the affluent, as the membership fee was a then extremely pricey fifty dollars.

These rules the club adopted in 1845 were as follows:

RULES OF THE HOT AND HOT FISH CLUB.
Whereas, the Club long known as the Hot and Hot Fish Club, of All Saints Parish, Waccamaw, was established for the cultivation of friendly

relations, we, the members thereof, with a view to perpetuate the same, do subscribe our names to the following Rules, for the regulation of the Club:

RULE I: Time and Place of Meeting.
It is the duty of members to meet, at or about 12 o'clock, M., at the Club House, at Midway sea shore, on each Friday, from the first Friday in June, to the last Friday, but one, in October.

RULE II: Admission of Members.
Any person, wishing to become a member, must be proposed by the President, and if elected by a majority, shall, after subscribing to the rules, and paying his admission fee of fifty dollars to the Treasurer, be entitled to all the rights and privileges of a member.

RULE III: Quorum.
Not less than two-thirds of the members shall constitute a quorum for the transaction of business.

RULE IV: Officers.
There shall be a President and Vice-President, to preside at the meetings, and a Secretary and Treasurer, to record the proceedings, and to take charge of the funds of the Club.

RULE V: Duties of the President.
Each member, in rotation, and in order of residences, shall act as President. He shall furnish ham, and good rice, but also attend to the preparation for dinner, to be on table at 2 o'clock, P. M., or not later than half-past 2. He must preserve order, and select sides with the Vice-President for games.

If absent, he must send his ham and rice.

RULE VI: Duties of Vice-President.
The Vice-President shall, in addition to his dish and wine, supply the Club with water and ice, and attend to the games. If the President is absent, the Vice President will preside, and his next neighbor officiate for him. He must also announce whether champagne will be brought at the ensuing Club meeting.

RULE VII: Duties of Secretary and Treasurer.
The Secretary and Treasurer shall keep a record of the proceedings of Club, take charge of the funds, receive or disburse, according to the vote of the

Club. He shall also keep an account of the debts due by, and to the Club, and furnish an annual report at the first meeting in October.

RULE VIII: Duties of Members.
Each member shall contribute at least one Substantial dish for dinner, also one bottle of wine, unless it shall have been previously announced that champagne will be furnished. He must also bring not less than two knives and forks, two tumblers, two wine glasses, two plates, and one dish.

RULE IX: Duty of Certain Members.
Each unmarried member shall be permitted in rotation to furnish a pudding, in lieu of that required under Rule VIII.

RULE X: Duty of each Member in Rotation.
It shall be the duty of each member in rotation to furnish sugar for Club for one season.

RULE XI: Prize Rule.
Should any member become the parent of twins, each member shall, in rotation, furnish one basket of champagne for the Club; the names of the twins to be announced after the removal of dinner, in an appropriate toast by the President.

RULE XII.
Whenever a member has an additional compliment to his family, he shall compliment the Club with a basket of champagne.

RULE XIII.
Any unmarried member who practically illustrates his preference to matrimony by being wedded, shall be complimented by each unmarried member, through the Club, with a basket of champagne, in commemoration of that event.

RULE XIV.
Any member of this Club, who shall be elected or appointed to any distinguished office in the State, shall for each and every such compliment, furnish for the use of the Club one box of champagne.

RULE XV.
Each member shall contribute annually five dollars, for the contingent fund of the Club, the same to be paid on the second Friday in June, to the Treasurer of the Club.

> *RULE XVI: Order.*
> *It shall be competent for the presiding officer, or for any member of the Hot and Hot Fish Club, through the President, to call the Club to order, during the introduction or discussion of any subject, and there shall be no appeal from the Chair at that meeting: any member persisting, shall be considered as severely censured by the Club generally.*
>
> *RULE XVIII.*
> *No alteration or amendment of the foregoing Rules shall be made, unless notice of the substance of the proposed alteration be given at a previous meeting, and the motion for such shall be renewed at the subsequent meeting, and two-thirds of the members on the roll of the Club shall be necessary to carry the same.*

Clearly, almost every rule in some way deals with epicurean delights, and the consumption of champagne was also obviously on the agenda for almost every special occasion. Yet for all the club's rules, perhaps the most important one was the rule that it passed to prepare for the eventuality that they saw coming long before it arrived: the Civil War. Rule XVII, added in July 1860, read:

> *RULE XVII. (Passed July, 1860.) Of Members absent from the Parish.*
> *It shall be lawful from and after the first day of August, 1860, for any member intending to be absent from All Saints Parish for more than one year, to acquaint the Secretary and Treasurer with such intention, and from and after such notice given, the said member shall not be liable for any pecuniary dues to the Club, until he shall, by appearing again at the Club, resume his rights and privileges of membership. But if a member shall be absent for a fraction of a year, beyond the first twelve months, then he shall not be liable for any dues owing during any part of that year. And members so absent, shall not be counted as members on the roll in cases where the Rules require a majority of two- thirds.*

Considering that quite a few of these men would serve, and die, in the Confederate army, this rule was no doubt adopted in anticipation of the contentious times ahead. Indeed, after the war began, there is no record of the club meeting again, and while some of the members served in local units such as the Waccamaw Light Artillery, many would become Confederate regulars and serve in the Tenth South Carolina Regiment and see duty in

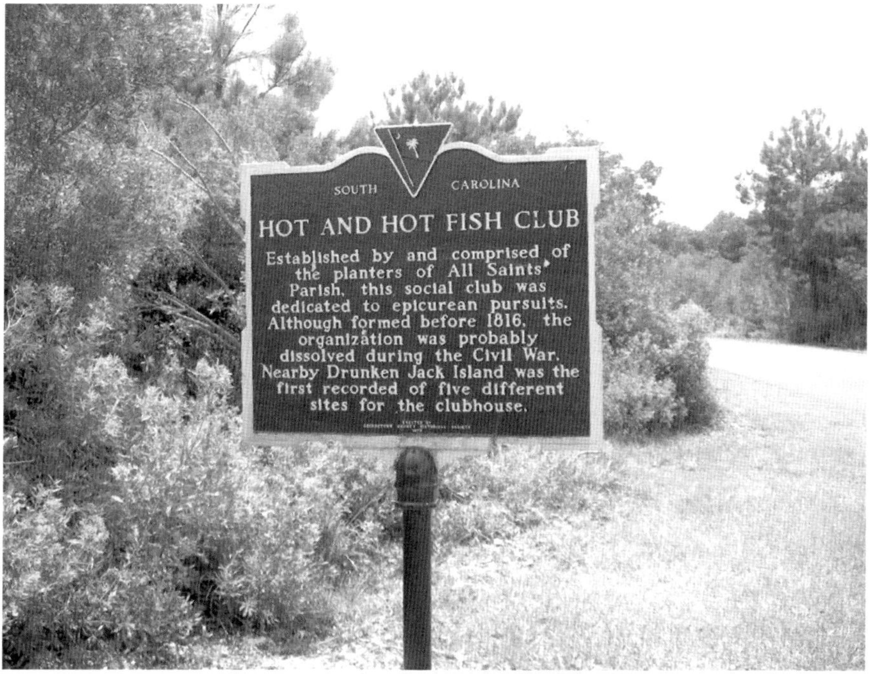

A historical marker at the north end of Huntington Beach State Park commemorates the founding of the Hot and Hot Fish Club and the first clubhouse on Drunken Jack Island. *Photograph by the author.*

the western theatre of the war, fight in Atlanta and later surrender in North Carolina with Johnston's army in 1865—at least the lucky ones who lived.

As for the magnificent clubhouse, the overseer of Chicora Wood plantation noted that in April 1865 he saw the clubhouse destroyed by recently freed slaves. Perhaps to those slaves, the clubhouse represented the oppression and misery they had suffered, and no doubt many of those same slaves had built the clubhouse, cleaned the fish and cooked, prepared and served the food. It mattered little that the clubhouse was destroyed, because after the war was over, the club's members were no longer the rich, carefree aristocrats of bygone days. Ahead was Reconstruction, and there would be little time for celebrating. Perhaps it was fitting that the Hot and Hot Fish Club disappeared along with the lifestyle it celebrated.

DRUNKEN JACK ISLAND

While the customs and procedures of the Hot and Hot Fish Club epitomize the gentility of the Old South, an outgrowth of this club was a myth that today is probably better known and even more colorful than the story of the Hot and Hot itself. That myth, the legend of Drunken Jack Island, may be endearing to children of all ages, but in reality it has no grounding in fact at all.

The "Visit Georgetown County" website offers the following brief version of the story:

> *DRUNKEN JACK ISLAND:*
> *Centuries ago, pirates quietly plied the inlet waterways to hide out and bury treasure. Among them was the notorious Blackbeard, who left behind a shipmate to guard casks of rum on an inlet island. When Blackbeard returned to the island much later, bones and empty bottles greeted him…and the legend of Drunken Jack Island was born.*

A local eatery named for the legend offers a similar version, though with a few more details. Its tale notes "that in the early1600s," Edward "Blackbeard" Teach and his men visited the Murrells Inlet area to unload and hide a cargo of rum. After burying most of the rum, the crew drank the remainder and ate oysters and other seafood all night. Waking up hung over the next morning, the crew sailed, leaving a passed-out sailor named Jack behind. The ship headed to the Caribbean, and only too late did the crew discover that their shipmate was missing. When the ship returned to the island two years later, all that they found were "32 empty casks of rum" and "the bleaching bones" of Jack the pirate.

It's a nice story—but one with no grounding in truth. The first thing that is wrong is the timetable, for Edward Teach wasn't born until 1680, so not only did he not live "in the early 1600s," he didn't age past his teens until the 1600s were over. He reached his fame as a pirate in roughly 1718, which was the year of his death. While he was known to frequent areas of the Carolinas' coasts, including both the region around Charleston and the Outer Banks, there is no record that he actually ever visited Murrells Inlet or any part of what is today known as the Grand Strand. It's certainly plausible, but there's no evidence that he or his crew actually did.

In addition, Jack the pirate would have had to be a poor pirate indeed to become stranded on what is today know as Drunken Jack Island. Located inside of Murrells Inlet, under the best conditions today at low tide one could quite possibly walk across the marsh to the mainland or the beach at what is now Huntington Beach State Park; under the worst conditions, a very short swim would be more than enough to get one off the island. Obviously, geographic conditions have changed over the last three hundred years, but as a small island inside of Murrells Inlet, at no time is it likely that the island would have been more than a stone's throw away from a nearby beach or the mainland. In that respect, no one who wanted to leave the island would likely ever find himself stranded there.

But these stories are irrelevant in any event, because the person for whom the island was really named was one of the original pre-1812 members of the Hot and Hot Fish Club, Jack Green. Green was a former Revolutionary War soldier, who South Carolina governor and Hot and Hot Fish Club member Robert F.W. Allston remembered as an immense man who stood "six feet four inches in his shoes, and weighed some three

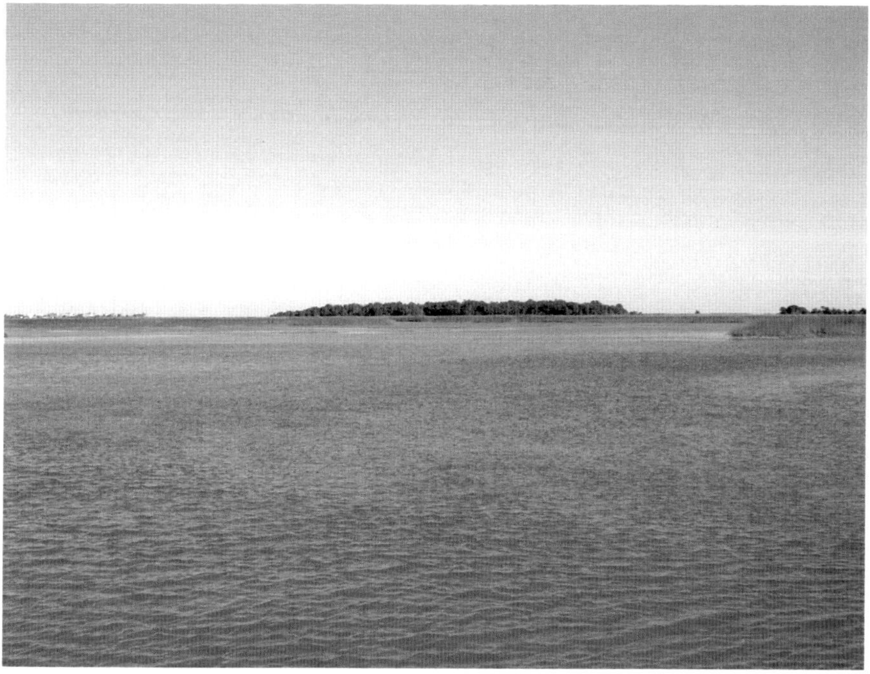

As this picture, taken from the mainland in Murrells Inlet, clearly illustrates, anyone who wanted to truly "escape" Drunken Jack Island (center) wouldn't have had to swim or wade very far—even three hundred years ago. Modern-day Garden City Beach is on the left, and Huntington Beach State Park is just an unpleasantly muddy walk (or maybe a short swim in shallow water) across the marsh to the wooded area on the right. *Photograph by the author.*

hundred pounds."Jack lived "on the sea shore summer and winter...his table being supplied, and bountifully...with game from the forest, and fish and shellfish from the salt-water creeks," and at the meetings of the club he was said to eat "a peck of fish at a meal, taking them in at one corner of his mouth and ginning the bones out at the other." Jack also had a notable proclivity for drink—he reportedly drank a quart of brandy at every club meeting—and because of his prodigious size, the "heavy and clumsy" Jack could be heard staggering drunkenly through the undergrowth on his favorite stomping ground, the island that is today known eponymously as Drunken Jack Island. Hence the name of the island, a name that stuck even though Green apparently "gave up brandy drinking entirely some years before his death" at a "good old age."

The Hot and Hot Fish Club, therefore, not only harkens back to the historical days of the prominent first families of the area but also represents the origin of a colorful if untrue popular legend as well. Obviously,

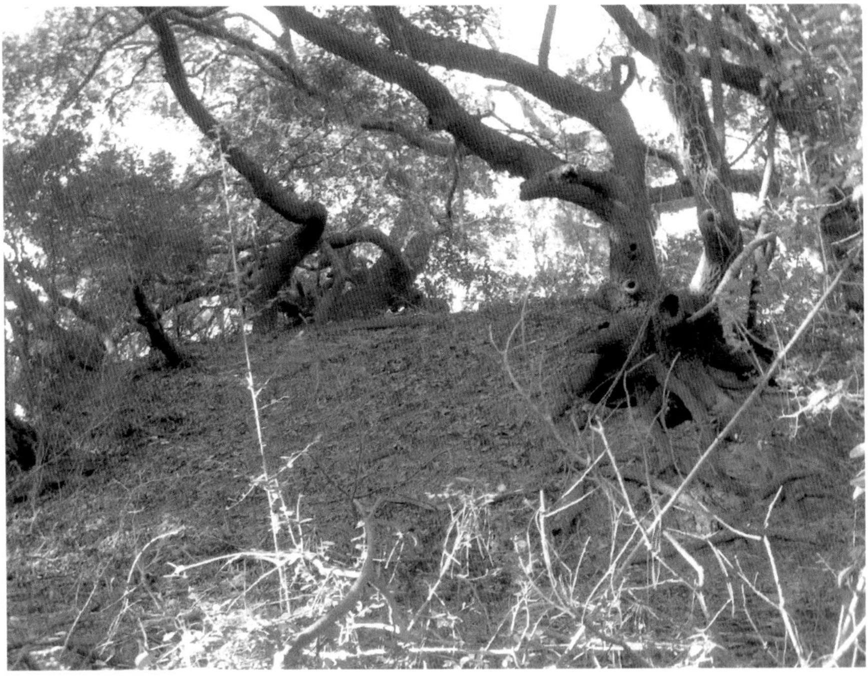

Though Drunken Jack Island is essentially a flat marsh island, there are massive earthen structures such as this one located in several places on the landward side of the island. These structures are of similar size and shape to Confederate parapets at other area locations, and the presence of structures that appear to be gun pits and powder magazines exist as well. In all likelihood, this was once the site of Fort Ward. *Photograph by the author.*

Blackbeard and his treasure make for a more interesting tale, hence the enduring nature of that story. Nevertheless, as a historical tale and as a myth, the Hot and Hot Fish Club and Drunken Jack Island add to the folklore and history of this colorful region.

But that's not to say that there aren't other, perhaps even more interesting historical events connected to the island. A trip there in January 2010 revealed not only several eighteenth-century nails but also .30-caliber machine gun shell casings head-stamped 1943—no doubt from the days during World War II when the U.S. Air Corps had troops stationed in Murrells Inlet and there was a crash boat base there as well. The greatest historical mystery connected to the island, however, is the question of whether it was the site of a fort during the Civil War. Confederate fortifications were built at a number of important strategic locations along the upper South Carolina coast, including Tilghman Point at Little River and at North, South and Cat Islands on Winyah Bay. Because Murrells Inlet's narrow, twisting waterways and island refuges presented access to nearby plantations, a three-gun battery named Fort Ward was also built in Murrells Inlet, and evidence suggests that Drunken Jack Island may have also been the location for that fortification.

Named Fort Ward in honor of planter Joshua Ward, the earthworks there apparently contained three guns and were initially manned by soldiers from Smith's battalion, which later became the Twenty-sixth South Carolina Regiment. A letter from Major William Capers White dated April 13, 1861, noted that he deployed "twenty six men and two officers" of the Waccamaw Light Artillery to Murrells Inlet and "twenty men and two officers" of the Wachesaw Riflemen to the redoubt at Murrells Inlet, though within a year the works were abandoned in a downsizing of the Confederate forces stationed in the area. Unlike documentation that clearly specifies the locations of other forts along the coast, in the case of Fort Ward, Murrells Inlet is as specific as the location gets. However, on Drunken Jack Island today there are a number of earthworks that are similar in construct to works built at the same time on Cat Island and works built later at Battery White. The Drunken Jack Island works are nearly identical in size and structure to those other works, and so although Confederate records do no more than name Murrells Inlet as the site for Fort Ward, it may be that the island was the location of yet another historical landmark in addition to the first Hot and Hot Fish Club clubhouse. In that sense, the island may actually be home to a historical site of even more interest and importance than a drunken pirate and a cache of rum.

Chapter 8

Myrtle Beach's Ocean Forest Hotel

Woodside's Utopian Vision

When analyzing the comprehensive history of the Grand Strand, there seem to be two distinct, noteworthy periods. First, there's the historical period from the early colonial days up until the end of the Civil War, when the plantations thrived and on the lower end of the coast some of the locals were among the most influential people in South Carolina and, arguably, in the nation. Judging from that period, the upper South Carolina coast would have seemed poised to be on a par with the Charleston area as a cultural and financial center for the state. However, after the Civil War, a once affluent populace fell into near poverty and the rice industry collapsed, and as a result many people would have argued that the area's better days were behind it. Unlike Charleston (which was more urban), the Georgetown area did not fare well in the postwar years.

North of Georgetown in Horry County, things were bleaker still. Even during colonial times and through the Civil War, the area that now encompasses Myrtle Beach had not been a particularly wealthy area, and in some ways it stood isolated and little regarded. Though it is hard to believe now, in the early 1900s a beachfront lot in Myrtle Beach could be purchased for a mere $25, and if one were to promise to build a house worth more than $500 dollars, the lot was free.

Even at that, few people were willing to settle so far from a major city and live almost isolated in an area where there were few decent, accessible roads. Consequently, from the end of the Civil War until the mid-twentieth century, on the surface there doesn't appear to be much of note that happened here, and until the tourism boom there was little to separate even

Myrtle Beach from any other sleepy little South Carolina town. That almost all changed in the late 1920s, and if not for a once-in-a-lifetime historical event, the development of the area might have taken a very different course indeed. Even people today people remember the primary catalyst for that change: the elegant Ocean Forest Hotel, which was the key element in the development that was to be known as Arcady, a utopian community that was never to be.

It all started with Greenville textile magnate John T. Woodside and his brothers J. David, Edward and Robert. John Woodside was a man with a vision, and even in the 1920s he saw the vast potential for this sleepy, isolated area that today draws upward of ten million tourists a year. At the time, Myrtle Beach had only a few hundred residents, and the Myrtle Beach Farms company was trying to sell land for development. The Woodsides believed that purchasing land in the Myrtle Beach area would be a good investment, and so they decided to purchase roughly sixty-five thousand acres for $950,000, a purchasing price that included twelve miles of beachfront property.

This was not John Woodside's first development project, and no doubt he was spurred on by two successful projects he'd already completed: the Poinsett Hotel in Greenville and Wildwood, a mountain resort in the Greenville area. Woodside's idea for Myrtle Beach was to build a resort area to rival anything in America at the time, and he would call that resort Arcady, named for a region of Greece in the Peloponnesus that had since ancient times come to be associated with Utopia. The centerpiece for Woodside's utopian resort community would be a hotel, and in addition to the hotel plans called for golf courses for men and women, a sixty-two-room clubhouse, a one-hundred-room beach house, stables, bridle paths, polo grounds, a yacht basin, playgrounds and camps for children and even an educational division so children visiting the resort wouldn't get behind on their academics. Arcady was planned and designed to rival any resort on the East Coast and to be as opulent as the French Riviera. Furthermore, in a real estate innovation that anticipated the time share boom of the 1980s, Woodside intended to sell family memberships to Arcady at the then very exorbitant sum of $1,250 apiece (adjusting for inflation, more than $15,000 in 2010).

Rhode Island architect Raymond Hood, who had designed the Chicago Tribune Tower, drew up the initial plan for Arcady, and Albert Allen Ainsworth of New York was named chairman of the overall project. Soon, landscape architects, engineers and city planners were working around the

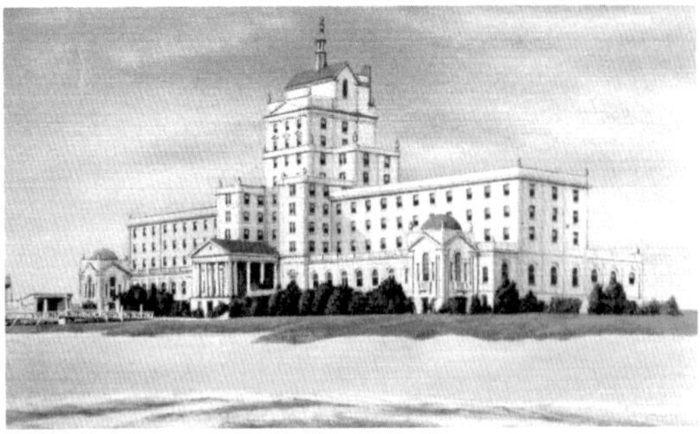

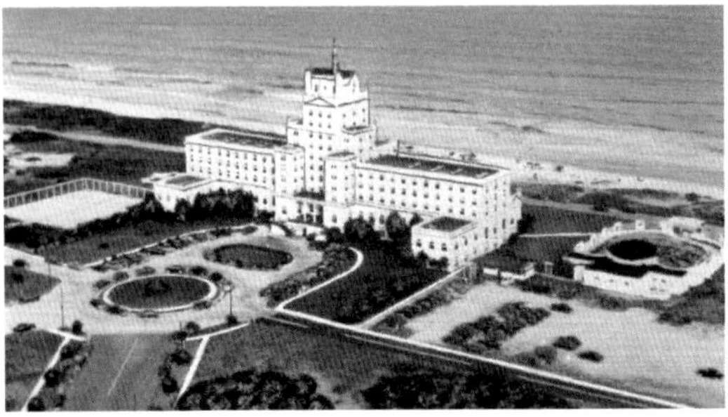

This page: The Ocean Forest's history is best told through the numerous postcards that featured the grand (and unique for the time and area) hotel. These very early postcards show how the hotel stood isolated early on but also how adjoining areas were obviously designed for the many features that accompanied the hotel. Some, such as the tennis courts and amphitheatre featured in the second postcard, would eventually be built, while other features, such as the yacht basin, would not.

clock to design the greatest resort the East Coast had ever seen. They began by paving existing roads and installing streetlights, and new roads were also drawn up and created. The construction of the clubhouse for the golf course began in 1927 under the direction of golf course architect Robert White, who would also be the first president of the Professional Golfers' Association. Hotel construction began in 1928, and the hotel was designed by Stanhope Johnson and R.O. Bannon of Lynchburg, Virginia. Named the Ocean Forest, but more often referred to as the "Million Dollar Hotel" (its reported cost to build), the building featured a ten-story tower in its center and was flanked by two five-story towers on each end. Sitting twenty-nine feet above sea level and well above the high-tide mark, the steel and poured-concrete structure would be considered virtually fireproof and storm-proof, and its 220 guest rooms and more than 300 rooms overall would reportedly make it the largest hotel between New York and Miami and, in fact, one of the largest buildings in the country. This edifice would anchor what Woodside considered the hotel section of Arcady and would be the focal point of the initial construction.

On February 21, 1930, the hotel opened its doors to a group of many of the most influential people in the East. The hotel's shops, exercise rooms, art gallery, indoor and outdoor pools, ballrooms, fine dining rooms, tennis courts, open-air amphitheatre, lush gardens and stables all impressed people who certainly

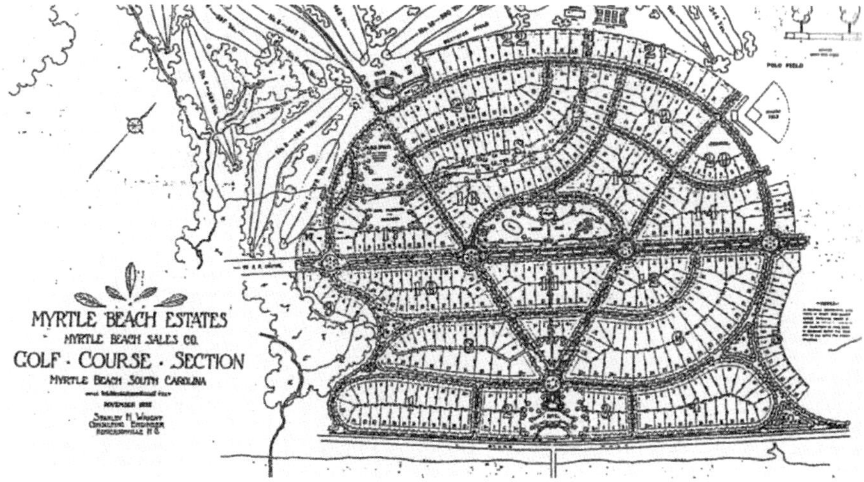

This plan, drawn up in 1926, shows the location of the Ocean Forest and the proposed layout for the surrounding Arcady community. Note the polo grounds at the top right.

knew the best and who knew that they were seeing it in the Ocean Forest. The hotel had elevators, salt and fresh running water, private bathrooms and ice water piped into each guest room. Italian marble Grecian-style columns, marble stairways, Czechoslovakian crystal chandeliers and Oriental rugs covering the marble-floored lobby all bespoke the elegance that Woodside's Arcady dream was to be. Evening dress and proper etiquette were de rigueur, as at night gentlemen were expected to wear tuxedos and ladies, evening gowns.

Even many of the hotel workers had an international mystique, as the managers of the hotel were originally from Canada and Austria, and other international employees included Dutch, German and Swiss waiters, an Italian chef, a houseman from Martinique and an Irish assistant manager. Hotel employees wore burgundy and gray uniforms, and Woodside's vision included the building of nearby residence quarters for the workers, which solved the problem of the lack of a local workforce, a problem that persists in Myrtle Beach to this day. It was truly a magnificent resort, and when it opened for the general public it would seem that the Ocean Forest's future would be bright indeed. The hotel was immediately booked up as conventioneers and meeting planners saw the Ocean Forest as *the* place to meet for business and pleasure.

Unfortunately, even before the hotel opened, fate dealt Woodside's dream a cruel blow. The stock market crash of October 28, 1929, and the subsequent Great Depression, affected a substantial number of Woodside's target clientele, and more importantly, the crash directly affected the Woodsides themselves. The Woodsides were ruined by the market collapse, and ultimately only the hotel and one golf course were completed. Woodside was removed as president of the Woodside Mills Corporation in 1931, and consequently, he was unable to make payments on the Arcady mortgage. His bankers, Iselin and Company of New York, tried to hold the property intact, but eventually investors purchased the hotel and the golf course and country club separately.

The new owners tried to remain solvent, and even though business was apparently good in 1930 and 1931, eventually the hotel was closed in 1932. Woodside had also defaulted on forty thousand acres of prime real estate between what is now Highway 17 and the Intracoastal Waterway, and this was sold to Charleston's P.O. Meade to settle tax payments that were in arrears. The Ocean Forest Club and its twenty-seven-hole course would fare better than the hotel in the long run. In 1944, it sold to Frederick Albert Warner Miles, and in 1946, he would sell eighteen of the twenty-seven holes to John McLeod, who wanted to develop the land for its real estate potential. Miles then hired Scotsman Robert White to redesign a new course by adding nine new holes to the nine he had retained. Known today as Pine Lakes International Country Club, the club is perhaps most noteworthy because, in 1954, a group of executives from Time-Life visited to play the famous course, and during their visit they planned what they envisioned as a new and important weekly sports magazine—*Sports Illustrated* magazine.

By 1933, the hotel was open again and the area was slowly growing. Pleasure boaters and commercial shippers were visiting the area more frequently with the opening of the Intracoastal Waterway, and by the late 1930s, Myrtle Beach was incorporated as a city and starting to expand. In 1940, the Ocean Forest was sold to John Stoddard and Lawrence Barringer, and so yet another change of ownership occurred.

The air force base in Myrtle Beach was established, and in the 1940s, it housed a sizeable military population, many of whom spent their free time dining and dancing at the Ocean Forest during the war years. Still majestic, the Ocean Forest was the ideal place for the rich and famous to come and play and the place that the common man and woman could go to see the rich and famous (such as F. Scott Fitzgerald, who was rumored to have stayed there in the 1930s), if they could afford it. During the '30s and '40s, the outside patio was the scene of a number of dances, and bands and entertainers including Guy Lombardo, Tommy Dorsey and Count Basie entertained revelers into

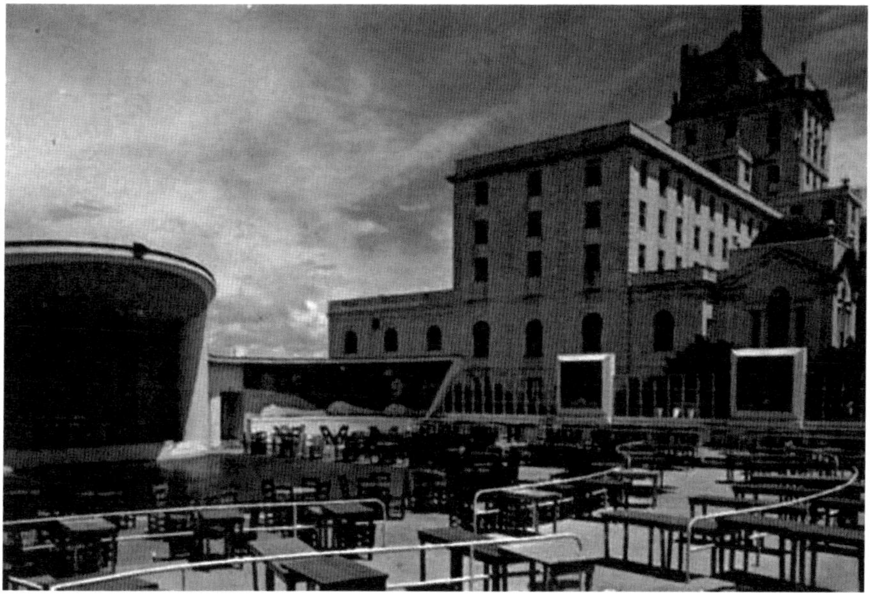

The Marine Patio was the site of performances by many famous artists in the 1930s and '40s, including Guy Lombardo, Tommy Dorsey and Count Basie.

the wee hours of the morning. On the "Marine Patio," partygoers could dance under the stars while brown-bagging their liquor, though not without paying for soft drinks and ice at a then expensive one dollar per setup. Summer stock performances in the outside amphitheatre-in-the-round entertained guests with performances by the likes of Shelley Winters and Brian Dunleavy, and the hotel was even home to the first area radio station, WMY13. The gleaming white hotel shone in the night, and the light that emanated from its beacon ten stories above the ground made it a presence even mariners far out at sea could locate.

Nevertheless, the hotel struggled to stay viable, and by the 1950s, the elegance of bygone days had faded into the more casually accepted lifestyle of the postwar years. Formal wear was replaced by more casual resort wear, and the hotel itself started to look tired and worn down. About 1960, the decision was made to sandblast the white paint off, leaving a less elegant red brick structure that looked not unlike a hospital. In fact, with the declining fortunes of the hotel, the Landcroft Corporation of Baltimore wanted to buy the Ocean Forest and turn it into a retirement home. That deal fell through, and many people were relieved because the hotel was still the only real convention site in Myrtle Beach. With the construction of the Myrtle

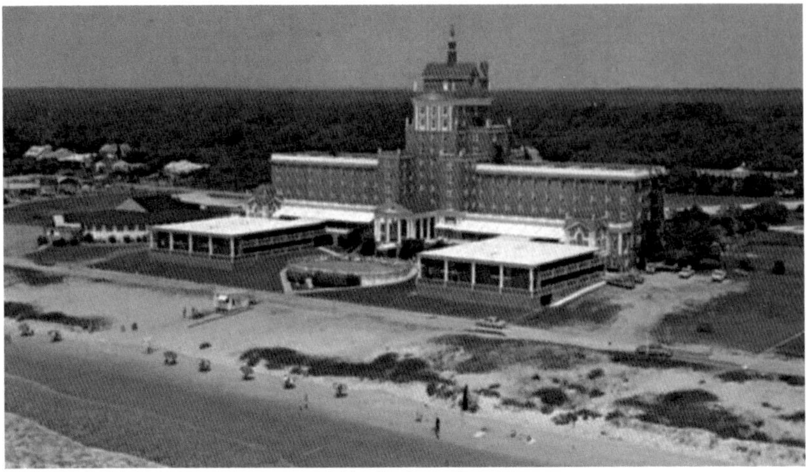

In the 1960s, the signature white-paint façade was sandblasted off the hotel. In retrospect, this only served to further strip the hotel of its once elegant feel and make the hotel look like an oversized chain motel. Convention space later added as wings also gave the hotel a more pedestrian feel, stripping it of its last shreds of grandeur and exclusivity. Perhaps mercifully, the then rundown and passé hotel was finally demolished in 1974.

Beach Convention Center in 1967, even that changed, and though motel-type units and more convention space were added in the late '60s and early '70s, this proved to be a bad idea because it detracted from the last vestiges of the hotel's elegance, which had been its main selling point.

After withstanding storms such as Hurricane Hazel in 1954 (which had wiped out many buildings on the beach, though it did not destroy the near impregnable Ocean Forest), the stock market crash, financial ruin and multiple changes of ownership, by the 1970s the hotel was in the last throes of a tortured existence. Niles Stevens and Dexter Stuckey purchased the hotel and the twelve remaining acres around it in August 1973, and the hotel encountered a final storm it could not ride out. Some say that the estimated expense of rewiring and replumbing the hotel to bring it up to code were cost-prohibitive, and others say the idea was to sell the hotel to a national chain, but after the deal collapsed, the owners couldn't afford to operate the facility on their own. Many people speculate that the beachfront property was simply more valuable without the aging structure than with it, but for whatever reason, the decision was made to demolish the hotel. On Friday, September 13, 1974, the hotel was imploded with the aid of dynamite, and forty-four years of history vanished in six seconds.

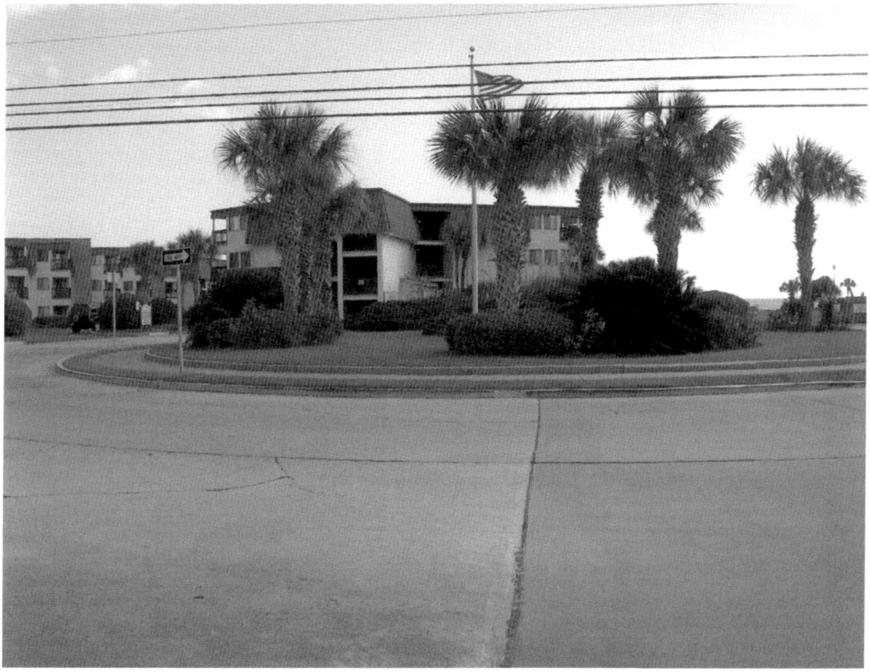

Sadly, today the traffic circle that once marked the entrance to one of this country's finest hotels is crisscrossed by power lines serving the ubiquitous townhouses that account for the typical beachside accommodations today. The roads that led to and from the hotel still exist, though they no longer pass by tennis courts and other amenities. No other trace of the Ocean Forest Hotel now remains. *Photograph by the author.*

Even today, though the structure no longer remains, the unique street layout of Arcady can be seen in the area of Myrtle Beach between Highway 17 and the ocean bounded by Fifty-second and Sixty-first Avenues North. There the V shape of the convergence of the roads, and the grand traffic circle that stood in front of the hotel, are all that's left to tell visitors that this was once an unusual area. It's a sad remembrance of what was one of the elite places to visit on the East Coast—a place that a *Sun News* article of June 20, 1974, called "a landmark and a symbol of resort life in Myrtle Beach." Though Arcady never became the utopian community the Woodsides envisioned, their dream of a place "where the leaders of contemporary life may sustain their capacity for work by bringing to its utmost the art of rest and recreation" did make a difference. For many people, it put Myrtle Beach on the map, and it did see the construction of the first major golfing facility on the Grand Strand, which became the cornerstone for an industry that today may well be the area's claim to fame, with over one hundred golf courses built in the last few decades. So despite the fact that the Woodsides' upscale dream was never fully realized—a dream that certainly would have meant that Myrtle Beach would have been more upscale and less a family-friendly tourist destination that it is today—it did mean, if only for a while, that Myrtle Beach came close to becoming the Palm Beach of the central East Coast and the most elegant vacation destination between Miami and New York.

HIDDEN HISTORY…OR MYTH?

The Ocean Forest Hotel itself has, of course, come to be regarded with a reverence of near mythological proportions, but many area residents have heard another tale about the hotel—that its ten-story tower held a private casino the likes of which has never been seen in the area before or since. According to legend, the presence of an illegal casino operated by Cubans allowed the hotel to flourish in the Depression years when business was lagging and the hotel was struggling. It's a myth that conjures up visions of the '20s and '30s, with gangsters and gun molls, a vision that is the complete antithesis of everything we know as Myrtle Beach today. But then again, the whole idea of the Ocean Forest itself is different from what we think about the Myrtle Beach of today. Did the casino exist? Are the stories true?

Apparently, in this case, there may be some truth to the myth after all. In Nancy Rhyne's 1981 book *The Grand Strand: An Uncommon Guide to Myrtle Beach and Its Surroundings*, she cites 1930s *Charlotte News* reporter Dorothy Knox's account of her visit to the Ocean Forest to do a story. Knox said that she knew firsthand that professional gamblers did indeed run a casino in the tower and that every game "from roulette to poker" was available. Despite the fact that it was the Depression, Knox said "money was piled on the tables like autumn leaves," and the place was packed with gamblers of all ilk in everything from "bathing suits to ball gowns."

If Knox saw these things, and wrote her story, then why does the question of gambling in the tower still exist as more of a myth than as not? "The men on the *News* loved [the story] and kindly explained they couldn't spare me for a material witness…[if] the joint was raided," Knox said, so the story was never printed. One suspects there was probably more to the suppression of the story than that—the hotel's clientele would have included a lot of influential people from some of America's finest families. And so the mystery of whether the tower held an illegal casino continues, even to this day.

Chapter 9

Waties Island, Fort Randall and Little River Inlet

Far from today's crowded beaches, on the northernmost point on the South Carolina strand sits an isolated bit of land that is one of the most historically important areas along the coast. As the one-time home to Native American settlements, a Revolutionary War encampment and the site of Confederate Fort Randall at Tilghman Point, today this nearly pristine area is home only to wildlife and solitude. But throughout the centuries, this land around Little River Inlet has seen a number of events of historic interest that have shaped the nation we live in, often at times when the landscape was anything but quiet.

While today Fort Randall may be the best-known (if little-known) point of interest in this area of just a few thousand acres, that fort was not the first site of historic interest in the area. The first brush with history centers on nearby Waties Island, which was the site of one of the oldest settlement sites in South Carolina. The island is named for William Waties (whether junior or senior is unclear), and during the early eighteenth century both father and son were in the business of trading with Native Americans, and both ultimately acquired large landholdings in several areas that are part of the region now known as the Grand Strand. Archaeological digs on Waties Island have discovered large Native American encampments from much earlier than this, however; in fact, mounds from as far back as the years 0 to AD 700 have yielded pottery shards and other artifacts. At one time, it is clear that this was a settled area long before Europeans even contemplated visiting these shores.

During the Revolutionary War, the area located a little west of Waties Island and south of Tilghman Point was a camp for anywhere from five to seven thousand colonial troops beginning in December 1776. General Francis Nash led an army from North Carolina heading toward St. Augustine, Florida, to keep British troops out of Georgia, and while on their journey they camped in the Little River area. Though they originally intended to camp in another location near the border, Colonel William Allston, who owned Waties Island and the surrounding property at the time, offered his land instead. According to accounts by Hugh McDonald, a private in Nash's army, this site was "a better camping ground, which was an elevated neck of land covered with hickory and other good firewood." Nash's army moved to the site on Allston's property and no doubt made at least a temporary ecological footprint, as the thousands of Continental troops camped and cleared more than one hundred acres of land in the process. They stayed there for about a month before moving toward Georgetown, and eventually to Charleston, before their orders to proceed to Florida were cancelled. Instead, they joined General Washington's army and fought at Germantown, Pennsylvania, in October 1777.

Though there are only scant details about these two early events, the role of Fort Randall and Little River during the Civil War is somewhat better documented. Even before the Civil War began in April 1861, the government of South Carolina planned and built a system of coastal defenses intended to protect the agriculturally rich areas of Horry and Georgetown Counties in the event of hostilities. Because of the region's system of rivers providing access to the interior of the state, once the war commenced the area was considered of prime importance not only to natives of South Carolina but also to the Confederacy as a whole. Plans called for fortifications to be built at Little River, in Murrells Inlet, near Winyah Bay at the mouths of the North and South Santee Rivers and on North, South and Cat Islands.

Logistically, the site at Little River for what would come to be known as Fort Randall was well chosen and easily defendable. Situated on Tilghman Point, a slight bluff overlooking Little River Inlet, the position offered a commanding view of the land and sea that revealed anything approaching for miles. The primary fortification was a wooden blockhouse surrounded by concealing earthworks, all of which were enclosed by a moat ten feet wide and five feet deep. Although these features made the fort easily defendable, more formidable were the cannons that the fort held in 1861. The Confederate objective early in the war was to build coastal strongholds and stock them with artillery pieces that would not only defend the district if needed but would also deter the Federal forces probing the area if they felt inclined to invade. Consequently, in 1861, Fort Randall's four artillery pieces—two

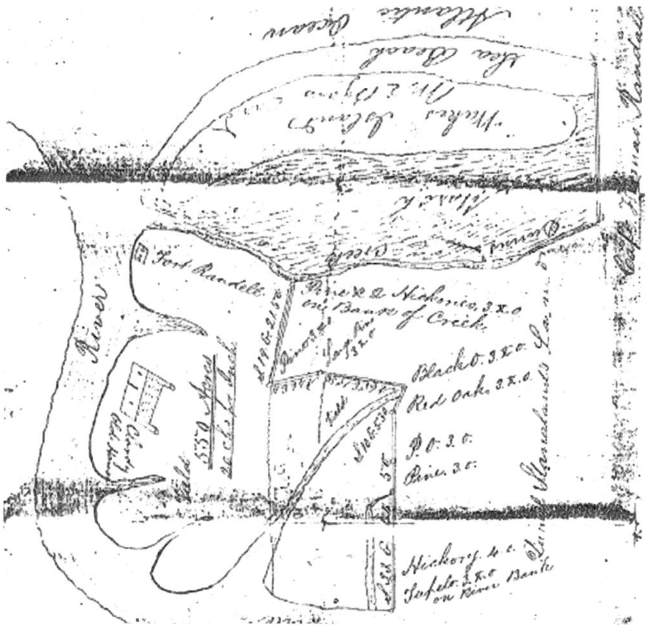

A November 1862 deed, showing Fort Randall, Waties Island (as "Wakes" Island) and the site where the Revolutionary War encampment had been located (in the area where it says "pine and hickories on bank of creek"). The deed registers ownership of the 550 acres containing Fort Randall and the Clardy House to Thomas Randall.

six-pounders and two twelve-pounders—were comparable in number to the seaside batteries on the southern end of the coast, where there were ten guns on Cat Island, five guns on the south end of South Island and the three guns in Murrells Inlet.

Because Fort Randall was the only major fortification on the north end of the coast early in the war, it is not surprising that the *Horry Dispatch* reported that the dedication ceremony in 1861 was an occasion of considerable fanfare, attended and presided over by local military luminaries such as Major William Capers White, Captain Thomas Randall, Captain J. Litchfield, Lieutenant L.L. Clements and Lieutenant T.W. Gore.

According to a dispatch from Major White to the Confederate secretary of war dated April 13, 1861, just one day after the hostilities officially began at Fort Sumter, the first Confederate troops officially posted at Fort Randall were thirty-three men and three officers from Captain Litchfield's All Saints Riflemen. Once the situation in the area stabilized, Major White would serve as the fort's first commanding officer, and the men in his command (from the Seventh South Carolina Infantry) would man Fort Randall until they were transferred out of the district and attached to the regular Confederate army.

The unit most frequently stationed at the fort during the war was the ubiquitous Waccamaw Light Artillery, initially under the command of Captain Thomas West Daggett and later under the command of Georgetown planter Joshua John Ward. In addition, "coast guard" patrols, though not stationed at Fort Randall, would often be deployed and shuffled from one area to another as needed. The first of these assigned to support Fort Randall were forty-three men and three officers of Captain Gillespie's Carolina Greys, who were responsible for patrolling the forty-mile area from Murrells Inlet to Little River in April 1861. Another unit that periodically fought in support of the troops at Fort Randall was the Camden Mounted Rifles, under the command of Captain A.H. Boykin. Even though the Camden Rifles unit was ostensibly stationed at Vaught's saltworks at Singleton's Swash in what is now Myrtle Beach, the Camden troops would greatly relieve the pressure on the thinly spread Confederate regulars in the district, and Boykin's men would patrol the beaches as far north as Little River, ultimately even relieving Fort Randall during emergencies.

As the war continued, however, trying to allocate the diminishing numbers of troops to the numerous forts along the Grand Strand would prove to be impossible, and most of the first-built forts would be dismantled within two years. Once Hilton Head capitulated, the Confederates considered a Federal invasion of the district unlikely, and therefore the forts in Horry and Georgetown were no longer considered key strategic posts. Consequently, twenty of the guns from the area forts were summarily stripped and sent up the Pee Dee River to the Northeastern Bridge and then transferred to railroad cars and shipped to Charleston.

The guns had not been the only things to go, however, as most of the forts in Horry and Georgetown Counties were degarrisoned and the troops sent to Charleston and other theatres of the war. Fort Randall alone of the original forts built along the coast would remain manned on a regular basis, but even at Fort Randall the artillery had been removed. Unwilling to leave the area so obviously undefended, however, the cannons at the abandoned forts including Fort Randall were replaced with "Quaker" guns. Yet even though it was still manned, the situation at Fort Randall was dire. Whereas in Georgetown troops could be shuffled back and forth between positions in a matter of hours when reinforcements were needed, when Federal incursions made Fort Randall untenable—as they soon would—support troops might take a day or more to arrive, if they arrived at all. The troops around Georgetown were often better supplied and better armed, and indeed when Battery White was built in Georgetown, it had anywhere from nine to fourteen guns in place at any time from 1863 on, while Fort Randall had been completely stripped of artillery by that same year.

Remarkably, though, at first the Union navy apparently didn't know how vulnerable the fort was, and even if it suspected it still showed it a healthy respect. One of the first official Federal military accounts mentioning activity of any type in the vicinity of Fort Randall was a report by Lieutenant George W. Browne of the USS *Fernandina*. Browne reported that on December 13, 1861, he witnessed what he believed to be more than forty signal fires along the coast at Little River, which he judged were guides for a blockade runner or runners attempting to come in. Based on the number of men he saw when he ran in closer to shore, he realized that "there was an encampment of Confederate troops and the distant fires were their picket guard." Browne explained that he opened fire with his starboard artillery and that in the darkness he could hear his shells strike some hard surface. Browne reported that he came around and fired on the Confederate troops again with shell and grapeshot. By this time, apparently, the Confederates had dispersed, and Browne had moved back out to sea.

Browne did not, however, try to run under the fort's guns, though he must have thought it odd that the Fort Randall's artillery had not returned the *Fernandina*'s fire. He, of course, had no way of knowing that the fort's guns

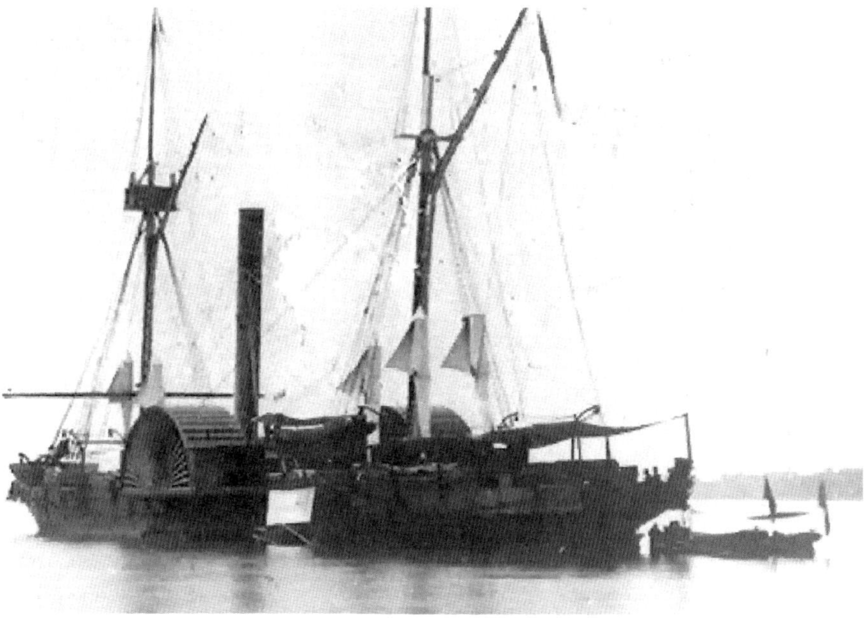

The USS *Maratanza* was attached to the North Atlantic Blockading Squadron during the Civil War and as such patrolled the waters around Little River Inlet and Fort Randall. *Courtesy U.S. Navy Historical Center.*

were just Quaker guns, and Union naval records show that it was only after Federal gunboats decided to mount an assault on the Georgetown island positions in May 1862 that they realized the artillery had been removed from the area batteries. Once the Union navy suspected that Fort Randall, like other area defenses, had no artillery, there was little to stop it from attacking Little River, and it acted fairly quickly.

On June 25, 1862, six Union boats—one each from the USS *Penobscot*, USS *Mystic*, USS *Mount Vernon*, USS *Victoria* and two from the USS *Monticello*—entered the inlet and went eight miles up to the town of Little River to destroy some blockade runners reported to be there. The citizens of the Little River fled when the Union boats approached, so the Federals worked unhindered as they destroyed two schooners, sixty bales of cotton, two hundred barrels of turpentine and fifty-three barrels of rosin. For several months, no further landings occurred, and the Union navy seemed content to blockade the area with only an occasional foray upriver, such as when, on November 24, 1862, the *Monticello* bombarded and destroyed two extensive saltworks near Little River Inlet. However, on December 30, 1862, runaway slaves taken aboard the USS *Victoria* informed the Federals that two blockade runners, the *Argyle* and the *James Bailey*, were anchored at Little River and ready to run out. A reconnaissance party from the *Victoria* attempted to land near the town to verify this information on December 31, but it encountered a patrol of Confederate cavalry from Fort Randall and was forced to withdraw. The party then proceeded upriver and attempted another landing but again stumbled upon Confederate pickets and was again forced to withdraw.

By this time, the Union navy was taking a keen interest in Little River; interestingly enough, though, the Confederates still considered the anchorage a well-kept secret. In response to a report by Confederate Charles Ost in October 1862, in which Ost lamented the lack of safe ports between Georgetown and Cape Fear, Major A.B. Magruder suggested Little River, as it "is not down on the charts nor on the coast survey, and its existence even—certainly its harbor and anchorage ground—is hardly known to any Yankee." One Yankee who did know about the anchorage at Little River was about to lead an assault on Fort Randall, and though unsuccessful, his efforts would point out the vulnerability of the fort and lead to further Union forays into the area.

On the evening of January 5, 1863, twenty-five men led by twenty-year-old Lieutenant William Barksdale Cushing approached the fort in three small cutters from the disguised blockade runner *Home* and the USS *Matthew Vassar*. Only nineteen when the war began, Cushing was the youngest man

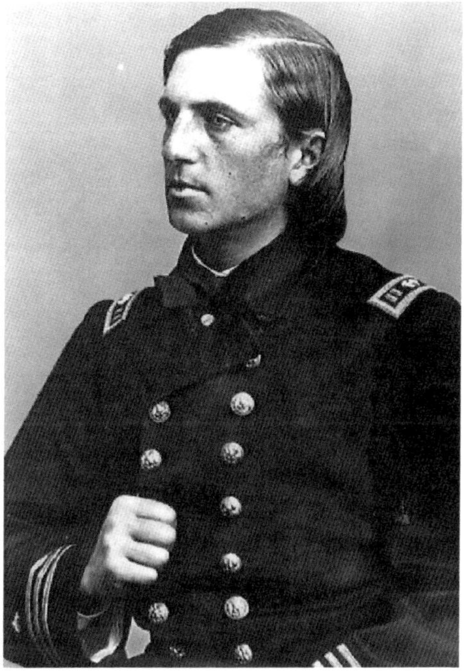

William Barksdale Cushing achieved the rank of commander in 1872, making him the youngest officer of that rank in the U.S. Navy. Despite his fearlessness and the appearance of invincibility he displayed time and time again during the Civil War, Commander Cushing's health rapidly deteriorated after the war. He died in the Government Hospital for the Insane in December 1874. He was thirty-two years old. *Courtesy U.S. Navy Historical Center.*

to achieve almost every rank that he held during the war. After starting the war as a master's mate in May 1861, he was made a lieutenant in July 1862 and would be promoted to lieutenant commander in October 1864. During the war, Cushing was at many of the most famous naval engagements on the East Coast, and already by 1863 he had been at the Battles of Fort Hatteras and Fort Clark in 1861 and at the battle between the *Monitor* and the *Merrimac* in 1862. His greatest fame would come after 1863, with the successful sinking of the Confederate ironclad *Albemarle* in 1864, a nearly successful attempt to capture Confederate general Louis Hebert and numerous raids on Confederate forts in North Carolina, among them Fort Caswell, Fort Shaw and Fort Campbell. Cushing's accomplishments would see him promoted to commander by war's end, and he would receive the personal thanks of the United States Congress for his role in the *Albemarle* affair. Cushing's daring and bravado made him well suited for the task of attacking Fort Randall, and on this occasion he would not disappoint.

Lieutenant Cushing and his men approached Fort Randall in their boats, and when they were about two hundred yards away, the Confederates spotted them and let out a volley of rifle fire. Cushing beached his boats and decided that his best course of action would be to form his men in a line of battle and take the fort. With their bayonets drawn and mounted, Cushing and his men charged the fort, "yelling like demons" he would later claim. Without firing a shot, the Federals stormed the works, "going over one side as [the Confederates] escaped over the other," Cushing noted. Initially, the rout was complete, as the surprised Confederates—a force Cushing perhaps optimistically claimed was "five times our numbers"—fled the fort while the Federals took possession of the wooden blockhouse. Cushing reported that the Confederates "left in such haste that their stores, clothing, ammunition, and a portion of their arms were captured." Cushing's men ate a hearty meal of pork and greens that the Confederates had left behind and then destroyed what they could not take with them and proceeded upriver. Later, Captain Boykin arrived with 125 men who had been stationed at Vaught's saltworks. The two forces briefly skirmished before the greatly outnumbered Federals ran out of ammunition, and Cushing had no alternative but to return to his ship.

Although their mission had been temporarily successful, the end result of the assault on Fort Randall was that the Confederates would realize how vulnerable the position was and thereafter strengthen their defenses at the fort. But the failure to take the fort would also serve as a lesson for Lieutenant Cushing, who would not forget the setback and who would one day visit Little River again.

Little more than a month later, on February 9, reconnaissance boats from the USS *Maratanza* captured a Confederate supply boat heading for Fort Randall. The boat was manned by 5 Confederate soldiers, and although 3 of them escaped before the boat was captured, the remaining 2 men provided the Federals with some very valuable information. James Gainey and George Smith, the Federal ensigns in command of the Federal boats, reported that they were told that there was one company of cavalry and one company of infantry stationed at Fort Randall, totaling 175 men in all. The Federals were also now in possession of some badly needed Confederate supplies headed for the fort: five rifles, a dozen blankets and twenty-three (of each) jackets, pants, shirts, hats, pairs of socks and pairs of shoes—supplies that the Confederates could not afford to lose. If the Federals had any intention of pursuing the 3 escaped Confederates, they were quickly dissuaded. Ensign Gainey noted that the escapees had by now alerted the troops at Fort Randall, "as we saw by their firing muskets and rockets." The information about the additional troops at the fort apparently served to convince the Federals that it was not a good time to try and retake the newly reinforced fort.

That didn't stop them, however, from probing the area, although one expedition in March 1863 almost resulted in disaster. On the third of that month, the *Matthew Vassar*'s Commander Hugh H. Savage sighted a large boat beached near the inlet and ordered Acting Master's Mate George Drain to take a party of seven men and destroy it. This was done easily enough, but as the landing party started back, it inexplicably turned its boat around and started to head up the inlet. Savage ordered recall sounded, but Drain's party paid it no heed and proceeded on up past Fort Randall.

Savage was confused and would become even more confused still. Lookouts on the ship had spotted Confederate troops coming out of Fort Randall, at which time Drain and his men had landed near the fort. Savage noted that he "fired two guns to call his attention to the boat's recall, and likewise to drive the rebels out of the woods where [Drain] was, all of which he took no notice of, but proceeded with his men into the woods, where I lost sight of them, and have neither heard nor seen anything of them since." At this point, Savage realized that his men had been captured by the Confederates, and indeed the next day Savage saw Drain's boat "with a quantity of Rebels in her," at whom he would lob shells to drive them out of the boat.

Once again, Federal troops who had landed in the vicinity of Fort Randall had met with failure, but on this occasion there would be repercussions. Captain Benjamin F. Sands of the USS *Dacotah* was so incensed at the capture of Drain and the men from the *Matthew Vassar*—under circumstances "so unaccountable…that it looks to me very like a desertion, or at best an act of recklessness without apparent object, and a great want of ordinary prudence and caution"—that he would order the *Matthew Vassar* relieved of duty in the area. A further twist on the story occurred on March 7, when the USS *Chocura* would be sent to Fort Randall and would report that another ship stationed in the area, USS *Victoria*, reported that "a large number of men in the fort…with a large flag flying and much cheering."

The *Victoria* began shelling the fort, forcing the Confederates out, at which time a Union sailor who had been concealed in the woods ran out onto the beach and signaled that he wanted to be picked up. This man was a member of the *Vassar*'s crew who had escaped capture and claimed that the reason the *Vassar*'s boat had landed was apparently in order to kill a cow for food. When the Confederates had surprised them, Drain had ordered his men to surrender to the Confederates, and in order to avoid capture the sailor dove into the river, swam to the other side and hid in the marsh. Captain Sands reported that the captured crew from the *Vassar*'s boat had been sent to Fort Caswell in North Carolina and would eventually be sent to Richmond to be confined as prisoners of war.

Later, after his release from captivity, Drain would claim that his boat was grounded on an oyster bed and that he was surprised by the Confederates.

Because his men had "no sidearms or bayonets, and but ten spare cartridges for their rifles," Drain said that he "deemed it prudent to surrender rather than have the men all shot down." Whatever the circumstances of Drain's and the *Vassar*'s failure, once again the Federals had suffered setbacks when up against the Confederates at Fort Randall.

Perhaps frustrated by their failure to simply drive away the Confederates at the fort, or because their attempts to have men in boats slip by or take the fort often resulted in disaster, the Union ships stationed in the area would content themselves with blockading Little River for roughly the next year, as well as stopping the blockade runners moving in and out of the area. Even before Cushing's and Drain's expeditions, the Union ships had encountered a number of blockade runners in early 1863, although those encounters had met with but a mixed rate of success.

The *Victoria* had captured the schooner *Argyle* on January 2, 1863, although the runner *James Bailey* was able to slip away in the confusion and run out. The schooner *Florida* had been captured on January 11, and on the night of February 20, the *Matthew Vassar* fired a volley across a blockade runner's bow, but the ship disappeared into the darkness. On February 22, the *Matthew Vassar* and the *Victoria* reported barely missing a steamer running out of the inlet and that later that same night a runner trying to enter the inlet saw the two Union ships on blockading duty and returned to the high seas. While these near misses must have been frustrating for the Federals, perhaps the most frustrating encounter of all came on the night of February 24.

A steamer trying to run into Little River came upon a patrolling Federal guard boat from the *Matthew Vassar*. Someone on the steamer hailed the soldiers in the guard boat, undoubtedly because they were unable to determine if they were friend or foe due to the darkness. The Federals in the boat replied that they were a Confederate boat and asked the runner's name—according to the Union sailors, the response was either *Hero* or *Arrow*. The Federals then shouted that they were coming aboard, and when they were within twenty-five yards of the ship they made a dash for the runner and tried to board it.

Realizing that it was a trap, the captain of the runner tried to escape, at which time the Federal soldiers in the boat fired a volley of rifle and small arms fire fore and aft of the runner and ordered it to stop. Nevertheless, the captain of the steamer opted instead for his freedom and renewed his attempt to escape. At this time, the *Matthew Vassar* came up in support and fired a broadside at the steamer, joined by the crew of the small boat, who fired two more volleys. The daring captain of the runner headed for the high seas, and owing to the *Matthew Vassar*'s distance from the runner and the exhaustion of the crew of the small boat, the steamer was able to slip out to sea. The captain of the *Matthew Vassar* signaled the *Victoria* to take up the chase, but it, too, was unable to catch the runner.

The *Victoria* fared better in March, when on the twenty-first it sighted a side-wheel steamer attempting to run the blockade. The *Victoria* and the *William Bacon* went in pursuit, eventually firing half a dozen shots at the ship in order to make it heel to. When it pulled up, it hoisted the British flag and, upon boarding, proved to be the *Nicolai I*, a blockade runner out of Nassau—though now a Union prize.

Little River was certainly no longer "hardly known to any Yankee"; in fact the blockade tightened, and there were fewer and fewer actions of note in the area other than an occasional report of a blockade runner captured or destroyed. Perhaps the Federals felt that Little River was sealed up well enough at this point that they simply needed to wait the Confederates out, and obviously, as a fort without any artillery and few troops, Fort Randall didn't present a formidable bastion that needed to be conquered in order to win the war.

Certainly from 1863 on, most of the more significant engagements in the area occurred to the south of Fort Randall and Little River. The Vaught Salt Works at Withers Swash in what is now Myrtle Beach would be scene of significant destruction, and Murrells Inlet would be the target of a Federal landing and bombardment. Most of the attention of the Union navy in the district would be drawn to the newly built Battery White on Winyah Bay, which, according to Union admiral John Dahlgren, was "a very formidable work," mounting sixteen guns. In light of these more pressing targets, Little River, which was relatively well bottled up by 1864, received very little attention from the Federals. By that same year, even the Confederate troops had apparently been removed from Fort Randall, as the Confederates seemed to realize the futility of manning a nearly defenseless and significantly less important position than Georgetown when troops were desperately needed elsewhere.

By 1865, however, mopping-up operations were beginning as the war wound to its inevitable close. Since the fall of Wilmington's Fort Fisher on January 15, the ships and men serving in the North Atlantic Blockading Squadron had been able to turn their attention to the smaller areas still in Confederate hands, and the Federals saw Little River as a piece of unfinished business. The man chosen to finally subdue Little River was Lieutenant William Cushing, and again he was to lead a small party of men into an

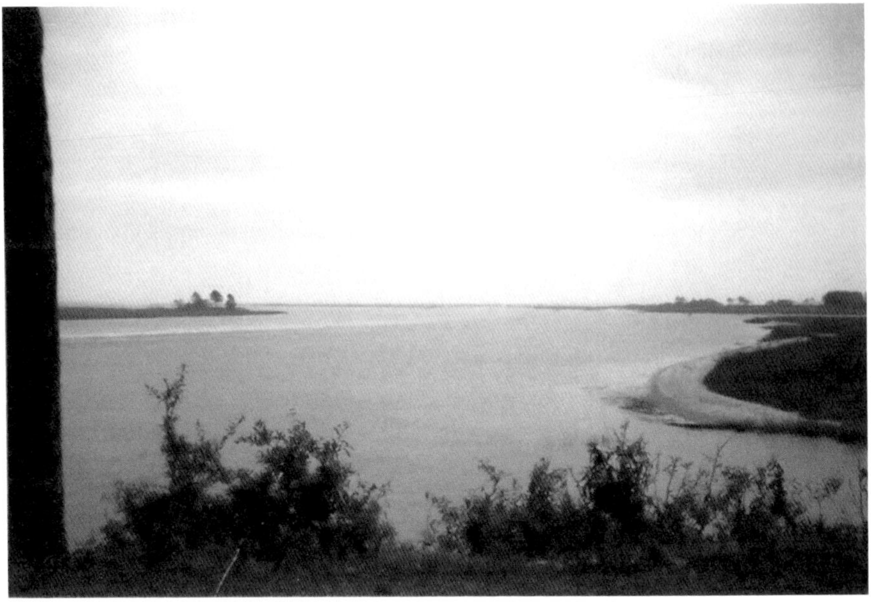

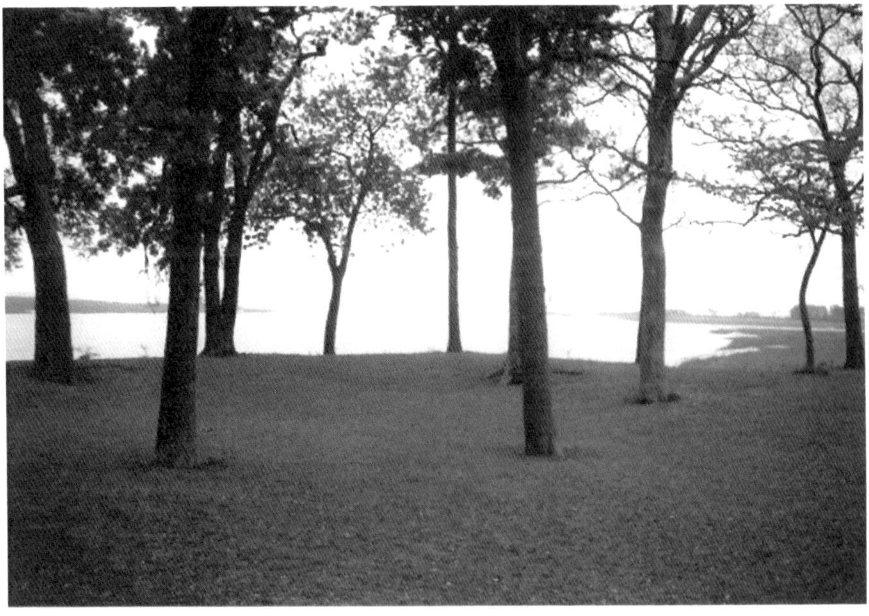

This page: All that exists at the site of Fort Randall today are the gently sloping mounds that were once part of the wall around the blockhouse. The earthworks have eroded over the years, but as these pictures attest, any Federal ships approaching Little River would have been spotted by troops at Fort Randall long before they were close enough to mount an assault. *Photographs by the author.*

enemy position—though this mission would be far more successful than the assault on Fort Randall in 1863.

On February 5, Cushing took fifty men in four boats from the *Monticello* and went up to the town of Little River. His men easily captured the town, as the few Confederates to be found there readily surrendered. After securing the town, his men destroyed an estimated $15,000 worth of cotton that was sitting on the wharves and slated to be shipped out. While his men occupied the town, he had occasion to meet some of the area citizens, and his observations about their attitudes were interesting. "The South Carolina planters, and all men whom I met, professed to be willing to come back under the old government," Cushing wrote, "and most of them seemed to be loyal men, only awaiting the emancipation from military rule." In any event, Little River and Fort Randall were now in Federal hands, and so it seems that the local residents had their wishes granted.

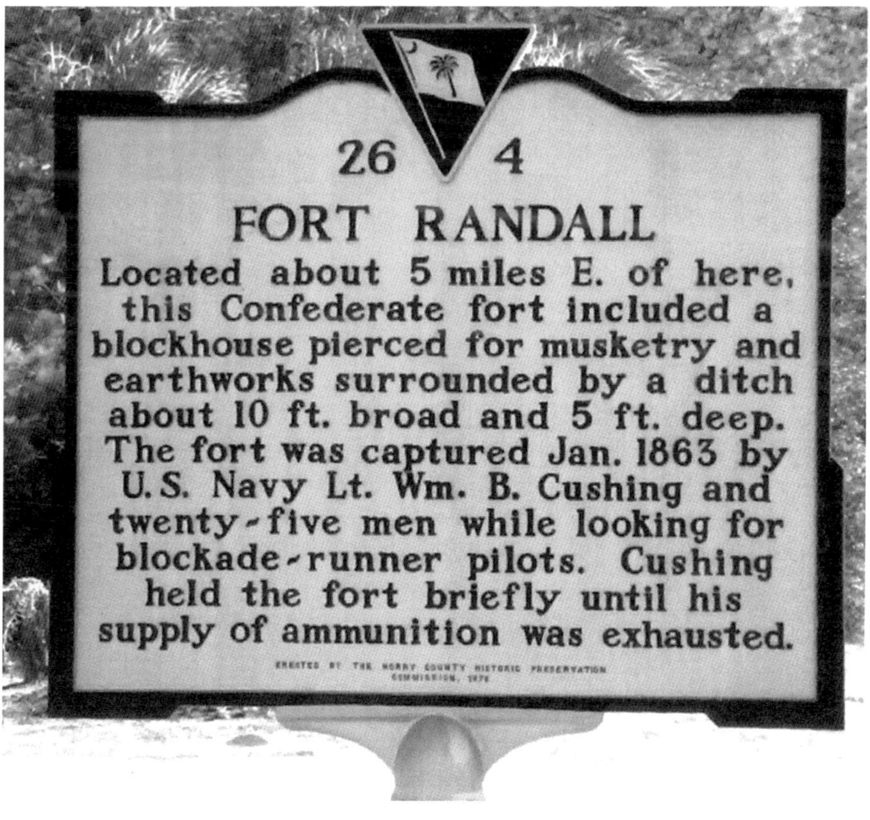

The Fort Randall historical marker, Little River. *Photograph by the author.*

After the war, Little River recovered much quicker than the other areas of the coast, which were dependant on rice and indigo for their economic sustenance, because the abolition of slavery did little to affect the fishing and shipping industries. In fact, period accounts note that just three years after the war, Little River was once again a bustling port, with ships regularly bound for northern ports, as well as the West Indies. Residents' love for and dependence on the sea for their livelihood have changed little since then, though Fort Randall, of course, has changed considerably.

Fort Randall's relative isolation is perhaps more apparent than ever, and the fact that it sits on private property makes it all but inaccessible. A historical marker on Highway 17 notes that the fort's location is about five miles to the east, and because the remains of the fort are now little more than gently sloping ripples in the landscape, there is little to see even if the visitor stands in the midst of what was once the blockhouse. What is most disconcerting is that over the past decade or so, the site has actually fallen victim to severe erosion and is in danger of eventually collapsing into the inlet. However, even today, the view from Tilghman Point is magnificent, and it is easy to see why it was chosen as a site for the fort; the position offers a commanding view of the land and sea. The same might be said of nearby Waties Island, and it—as well as the fort and the site of General Nash's colonial army encampment today—rests undisturbed as former witnesses to a remarkable number of nation-shaping historical events and periods.

Chapter 10

Four Grand Strand Landmarks that Disappeared Before their Time

For every well-known site of historical interest that exists in the area today, there are dozens more that have disappeared with barely a trace. In many cases, the general location of these places can be identified, but in other instances, there may be almost nothing left to help locate the missing landmarks. This may be especially true of places that may not have been seen, at the time, as being of major, long-term historical importance, and indeed that is understandably true of some of the places that will be discussed in this chapter. Nevertheless, we continue to hear about these places again and again—if for no other reason, that makes these sites worth revisiting here. While a number of these types of landmarks have existed in this area at one time or another, those significant enough to bear mentioning here are the Washington Park Racetrack, Hurl Rocks, the Pawleys Island Pavilion and the Myrtle Beach Prisoner of War Camp.

The Washington Park Racetrack

In the 1930s, the future that was mapped out for Myrtle Beach must have indeed seemed quite different from the result that we see now. With the opening of the elegant Ocean Forest Hotel, as well as the establishment of Robert Woodside's Arcadia community, the area seemed to be developing into an resort destination that would appeal to an urbane and sophisticated international crowd, who would be looking for entertainment in addition to the beaches, golf and tennis courses and polo fields. Thus, the Washington

Park Racetrack must have seemed to be a high-end diversion that was exactly what the area needed.

In 1938, Paul and Parrot Hardy of Mullins, South Carolina, opened the Washington Park Racetrack at what is now Twenty-first Avenue North and Oak Street in Myrtle Beach, much of which is today located under the parking lot of another former area landmark, the Myrtle Square Mall. When it opened in June of that year, the park had grandstands that seated more than 5,000 people (they were full on opening day and included the South Carolina governor), and a mile-and-a-half-long track offered harness racing several days a week. Built at the not-insignificant cost of $40,000, the track offered superb views not only of the track but of the ocean as well. No doubt this type of entertainment appealed to the Ocean Forest's clientele, and for more than a decade the races were entertainment for large crowds (on the average, more than 2,500 a week) seeking diversion. In *Myrtle Beach: A History, 1900–1980*, Barbara Stokes notes that in 1939 more than "fifty horses from five states were stabled at the track." Postcards from the 1930s and '40s show packed bleachers and well-dressed crowds watching the races.

Just as the area would never be able to fully sustain the Ocean Forest Hotel despite periods of success, the same was true of the Washington Park track. By 1947, the track had closed, but not because of a lack of interest—during the war the crowds had probably been as strong as ever—but because the state had decided not to legalize parimutuel gambling. Although gambling was not legal in South Carolina, state-regulated parimutuel gambling had been seriously considered, as is the case in some other states where dog and horse racing is a state-sanctioned type of gambling. After the final failure of the legalized gambling bills (although, as recently as this decade, attempts have been made to legalize gambling), the track was closed. Efforts were made in the early 1950s to revive the track with weekly races, but because betting was illegal, the effort was doomed to failure.

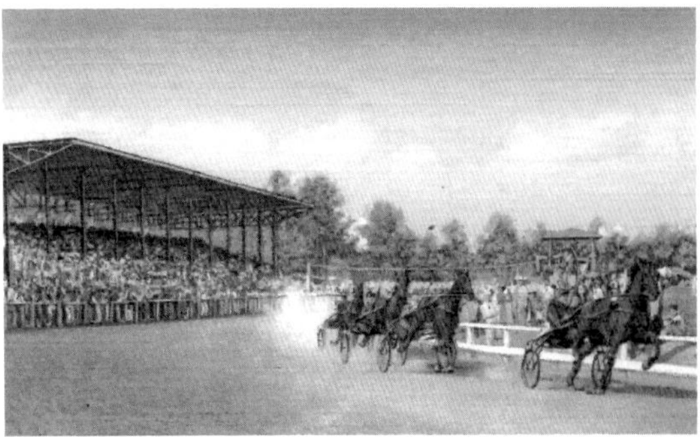

Postcards from the 1930s and '40s emphasized large, fashionable crowds at the Washington Park Racetrack, even more so than the harness races themselves.

Despite the fact that the track no longer exists, reportedly a vegetal outline of a part of the track and park is still visible from the air at the site of the Wachovia National Bank on Oak Street in Myrtle Beach.

THE PAWLEYS ISLAND PAVILIONS

Almost unique among the many vanished Grand Strand landmarks is the Pawleys Island Pavilion (or Pavilion*s*, as the case really stands). These places were so revered, and their mention evokes so much nostalgia, that even today annual festivals are held and thousands of people have gathered to celebrate just the *memory* of the Pawleys Island Pavilion. No pavilion has existed at Pawleys Island in any form since the 1970s, yet to this day images of the pavilions can be found throughout the coastal region. The many incarnations of the pavilions and their ultimate demise make for a tale worth telling.

The first pavilion on Pawleys Island was apparently built in the early 1900s and was a wooden structure that was located among the dunes on the island

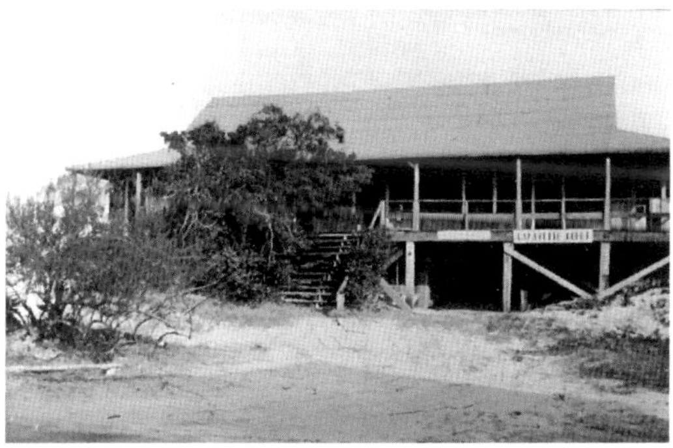

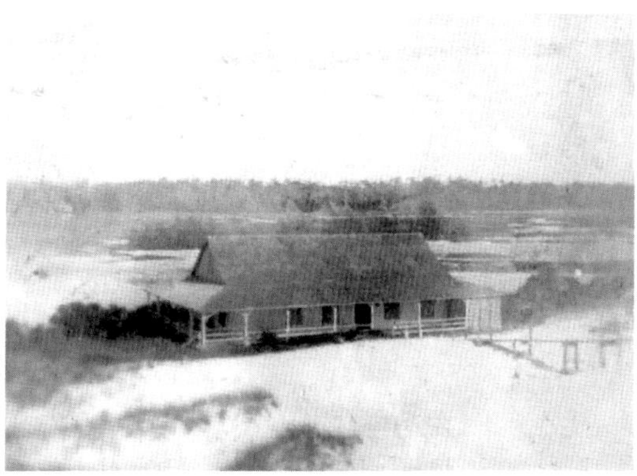

This page: The picture above, taken about 1925, shows the first Pawleys Island Pavilion shortly after it was purchased and converted to a rental property. The picture below, also from about 1925, shows the second pavilion, which replaced the first. *Courtesy Pawleys Island Civic Association and the Georgetown County Digital Library.*

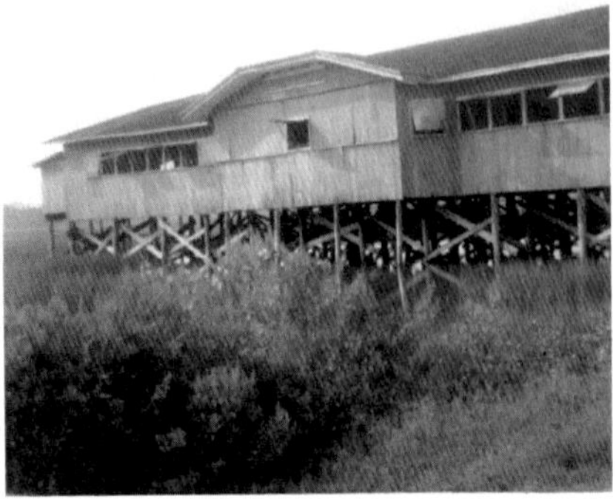

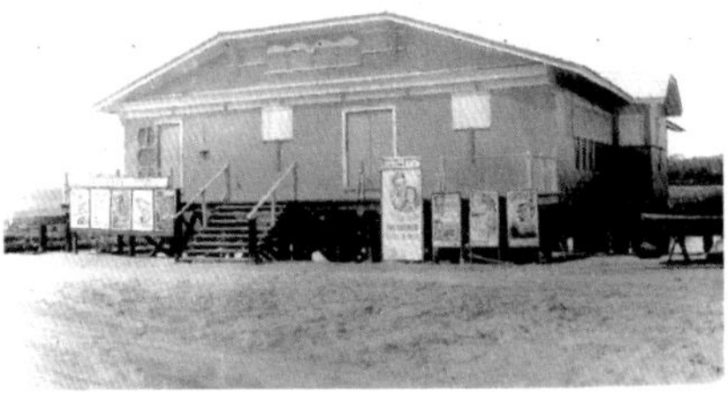

This page: Pavilion III (top), also known as the Lafayette Pavilion, viewed from the marsh and the front. The pavilion was built about 1935, and as the site today shows (bottom), only a marker now remains. *Top Photographs courtesy Pawleys Island Civic Association and the Georgetown County Digital Library; bottom photograph by the author.*

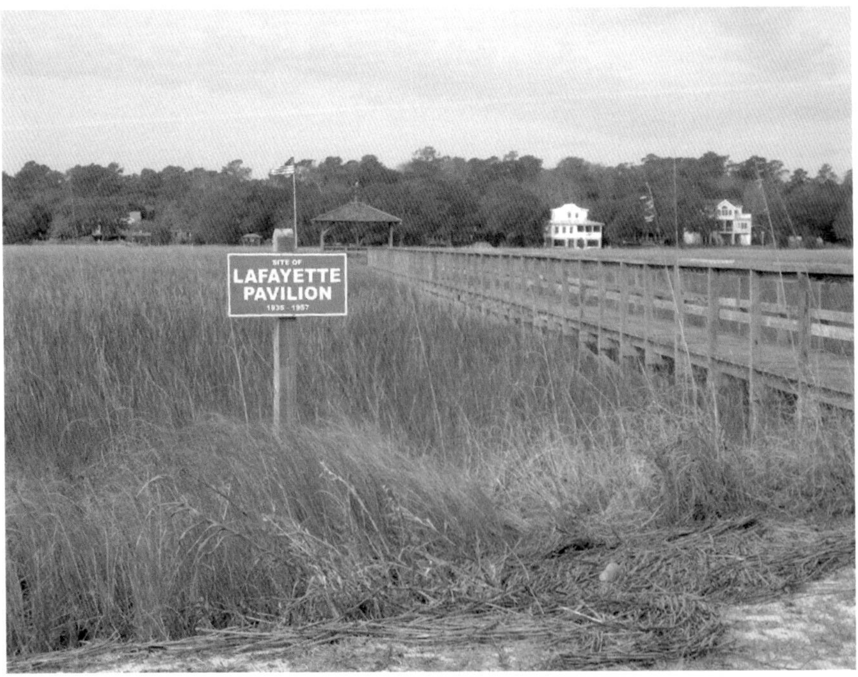

north of the South Causeway. In this and the pavilions that followed, the main activities at the pavilion were dancing and drinking, although during Prohibition, obviously, the only drinking that was supposed to be going on was the sale of soft drinks and the like. Nevertheless, local folklore has it that even then one could enjoy an alcoholic libation if you knew the right people and if the price was right.

Eventually, the first pavilion was converted to a cottage, and a second pavilion was built nearby by Willie Lachicotte in 1925. This simple structure, with wooden floors and no restrooms, was built just north of the first pavilion. During the summer, bands would play in this pavilion, but it wasn't until the third pavilion was built that the bands would become a truly integral part of summer at the Pawleys Pavilion. This third pavilion, which was built by Fred Brickman in 1935 near the South Causeway, would be known as the Lafayette Pavilion. This pavilion would be a mainstay of summer activity on the island, even though it was unable to open at night during World War II because of blackout conditions. It was after this pavilion burned down in 1957 due to a faulty electrical system that the most famous pavilion of them all was built in 1960, the pavilion on the marsh at the North Causeway.

Funded by a group of local people who were nostalgic for the previous pavilion, Georgetown senator James Morrison apparently even had the triangle road built at the site to provide a location for the structure. This large wooden structure had a huge dance floor and booths around the walls and soon became *the* place to be on the south end of the coast. From 1960 until 1970, some of the most popular regional bands (and some known even on a national scale) played at this site, and the band names are especially familiar to aficionados of the Carolina Beach Music sound. The Drifters, the Caravelles, the Monzas, Maurice Williams and the Zodiacs, the Catalinas, the Rivieras, the Embers, the Esquires and many others played there, drawing crowds of hundreds of people who enjoyed good music, cold beer and a safe and nearby place to relax and have a memorable summer evening. One of the most interesting attributes of this building was that customers, as well as the bands that played there, were invited to sign their names in and on the building, and this is obvious in many of the period photographs of the structure.

Unfortunately, the good times were not to last. In June 1970, the pavilion was mysteriously burned down by an arsonist, and many suspect that it was because some area residents feared that the pavilion was becoming *too* popular and as such was drawing in too many outsiders and therefore might eventually attract the "wrong crowd." Though there were plans to

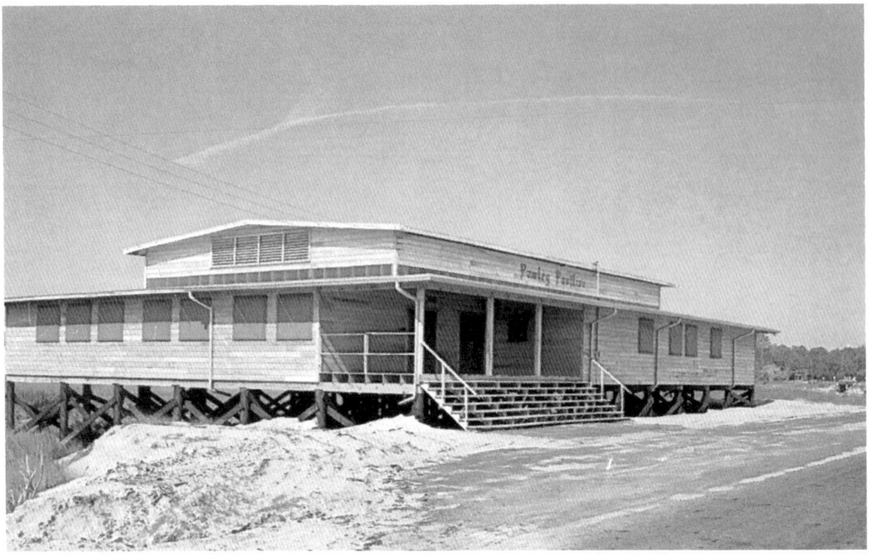

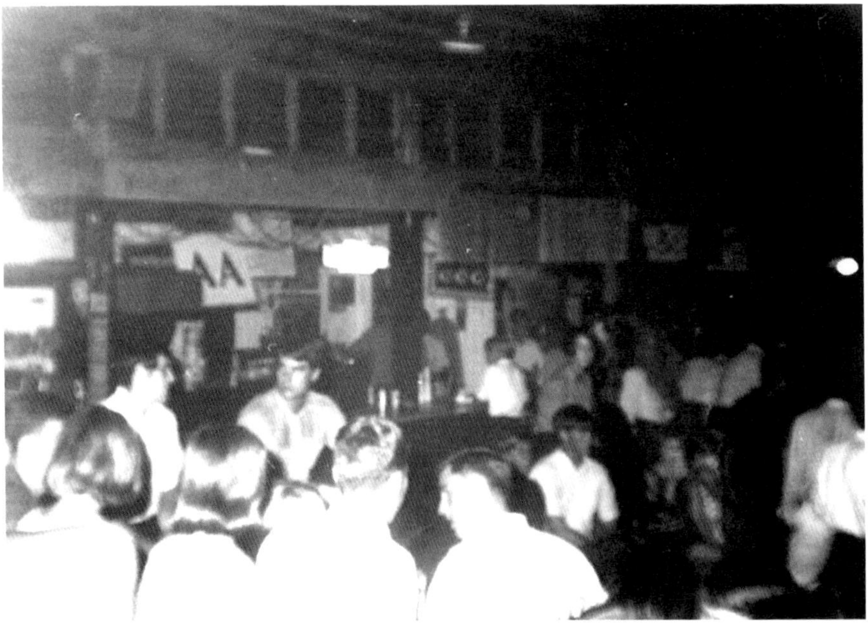

This page: The most famous pavilion of them all, Pavilion IV, drew large crowds every night. Perhaps its popularity led to its mysterious destruction in 1970. *Courtesy Pawleys Island Civic Association and the Georgetown County Digital Library.*

convert a nearby structure into what would have been a fifth pavilion, some area residents, who had apparently had enough, bought that structure and razed it.

Today, annual spring festivals in Pawleys Island celebrate the summers spent at this last pavilion, but truth be told, the celebration really revels in the spirit of all of the pavilions. Real estate on the island is far too pricey for the construction of this type of commercial structure today, and furthermore, local residents have worked hard to ensure that the island remains the one pristine stretch of beach on the South Carolina coast, untainted by commercialism and devoid of attempts make it anything more than a family-friendly beach. That's probably a good thing, though no doubt many Pawleys residents would love to walk over to the pavilion for a cold beer and to listen to some beach music.

HURL ROCKS

This site apparently was named for an English settler named Hearl, perhaps simply because he lived closest to what was an unusual geologic formation of black rocks that was once a popular destination for many tourists and locals in the area, who were curious to see the isolated outcropping of two-million-year-old rocks on the sandy shore of Myrtle Beach. The only naturally occurring rocks on the South Carolina coast, they were noted by eighteenth-century naturalists John and William Bartram on their travels through the Southeast. Described by Bartram as "so soft" that a sharp knife could cut holes in them, this outcropping of rocks—once actually described as a cliff—existed at what is now Twenty-first Avenue South at Ocean Boulevard in Myrtle Beach.

The site was a popular destination for picnics and beach parties, and in the early twentieth century the rocks still stood as high as six feet above the sand. By the twentieth century, the name "Hearl Rocks" had become "Hurl Rocks," and the park at the site bears this more modern name. Today, a plaque exists honoring the Bartrams and their discovery, as well as other signage designating Hurl Rock Park, but the rocks themselves can no longer be seen. Once a staple subject for the local tourist postcard and brochure industry, like other area items of interest that once lay on the beach—such as the shipwrecks of the *Freeda A. Wyley* and the *Jonathan May*—the Hurl Rocks were covered by the extensive beach renourishment projects of the 1990s. Many residents, however, hope that the next big storm may once again expose the rocks and bring to the surface one of the Grand Strand's most unusual landmarks.

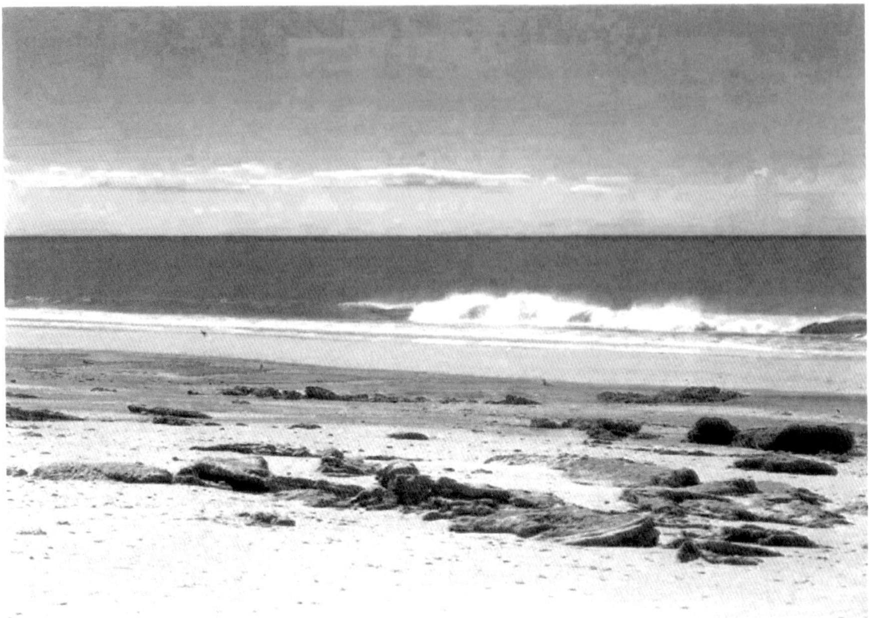

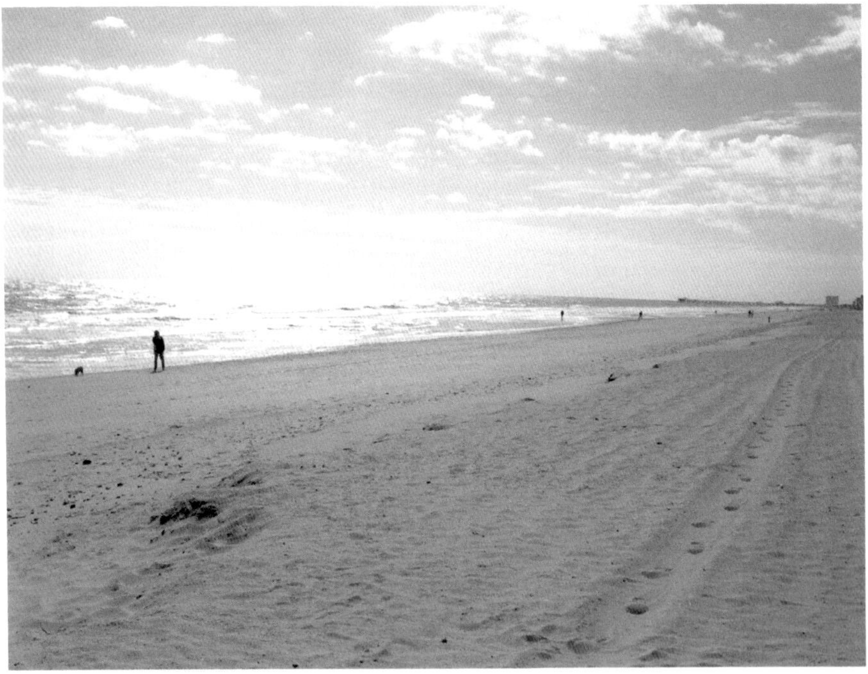

This page: As the top photograph from the 1960s shows, the beach known as Hurl Rocks was once strewn with rocks that had, at one time, been as high as six feet. As the picture from 2010 shows, the rocks are now completely covered.

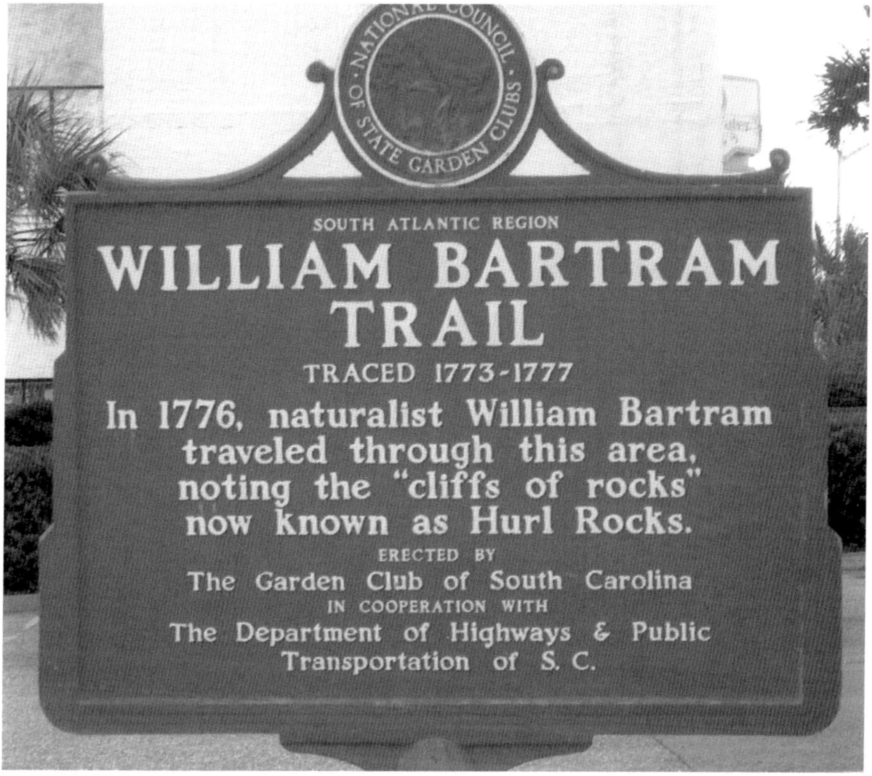

A marker at Hurl Rocks Park in Myrtle Beach commemorates William Bartram's visit, though sightseers may be puzzled as to why the marker mentions "cliffs of rocks" when no cliffs or rocks are present. *Photographs by the author.*

THE MYRTLE BEACH PRISONER OF WAR CAMP

Perhaps nothing is more incongruous with the idea of the sun, sand and surf than the reality that Myrtle Beach once had a camp for German POWs. Indeed, during World War II the first camp in this area was one of eight temporary camps in South Carolina and housed as many as six hundred German prisoners in the area near Cane Patch Swash that stretched from the beach to Highway 17 between Seventy-first and Seventy-ninth Avenues North in Myrtle Beach. The men in this camp were put to use performing various tasks of manual labor in the area but most notably to cut pulpwood. They were also used to assist in the building of barracks on the Myrtle Beach Air Base, and they were eventually moved to a more permanent facility, which would be one of the twenty permanent South Carolina POW camps that housed more than eight thousand prisoners by 1944 and more than eleven thousand at their peak. One official noted of the Myrtle Beach camp: "I could not help but think of a Boys Summer Camp in which I used to spend my vacation; the same beautiful trees, same seclusion, same quietness of the woods, and similar barracks, too."

The first German prisoners sent to South Carolina were put to work harvesting peanuts, but in Myrtle Beach, they initially grew tobacco in addition to cutting pulpwood; when in 1945 the Pee Dee River flooded, many of the POWs from Myrtle Beach helped rebuild and repair the many bridges that had washed out. Though they were far from home, there were a few escape attempts, though apparently all of the escapees were later apprehended. There were no violent uprisings (as a precautionary measure, the United States government had the most hardcore Nazi prisoners sequestered together in Camp Alva, Oklahoma, which no doubt led to fewer incidents in the other camps), and only two of the prisoners died here in Myrtle Beach, one of whom drowned swimming in the ocean and who is now buried at the Ocean Woods Cemetery, and another who committed suicide at the end of the war after learning that Germany had been defeated. By 1946, all of the German prisoners in the state had been returned to Germany.

The first, temporary camp had been dismantled after the prisoners had moved to the permanent facility, and no trace of this camp remains in what is now a well-developed area. The second camp was absorbed into the air base, but in the 1990s the Myrtle Beach Air Force Base was closed and is currently being developed for high-end commercial and residential property. In this case, the Myrtle Beach Prisoner of War Camp is a historical site that vanished without a trace and without a piling, earthwork or plaque to mark the spot.

Bibliography

"Battery White." http://batterywhite.org.

Brevard, Joseph. *An Alphabetical Digest of the Public Statute Law of South Carolina.* Charleston, SC: Hoff, 1814.

Broach, Jackie. "The Search for Some Early Visitors" *Coastal Observer* (2009), 6.

Bryant, Dawn. "Grand Hotel Set Stage for Recent Upscale Development in Myrtle Beach." *Sun News*, September 13, 2004.

Burroughs, Ben. "Revolutionary War Encampment." http://ww2.coastal.edu/ben/other/RevolutionaryWarEncampmen.pdf.

———. "Waties Island History." http://ww2.coastal.edu/ben/other/WaitesIslandHistory.pdf.

Chase, Eugene, and Richardson, Katherine. *Pawleys Island: Historically Speaking.* Pawleys Island, SC: Pawleys Island Civic Association, 1994.

Clary, Margie Willis, and Kim McDermott. *Images of America: South Carolina Lighthouses*. Charleston, SC: Arcadia, 2008.

Coastal Observer. "Researchers Hunt Spanish Shipwreck." August 28, 2008.

Coast magazine 29, no. 20. "Shipwrecks Along the Grand Strand" (July 8, 1984): 12–13, 22.

County Historical Society website. http://hchsonline.org.

Craigle, Janel. "The Ocean Forest Hotel: A Glimpse from the Past." *Alternatives* magazine (n.d.).

Dabbs, James Mcbride. *Pee Dee Panorama*. Columbia: University of South Carolina Press, 1951.

Department of the Navy. "Naval Historical Center." http://www.history.navy.mil/branches/nhcorg11.htm.

Dozier, Jamie. E-mail messages to author on North Island, September 14, 2009, and January 28, 2010.

Evans, Clement A. *Confederate Military History: South Carolina*. Atlanta, GA: Blue and Gray Press, 1899.

Floyd, Blanche W. *Tales Along the Grand Strand of South Carolina.* Winston-Salem, NC: Bandit, 1996.

———. *Tales Along the Kings Highway of South Carolina.* Winston-Salem, NC: Bandit, 1999.

———. "When the POWs Came." *Myrtle Beach* magazine (n.d.): 24–25.

Georgetown County Digital Library. http://www.gcdigital.org/index.php.

Helgason, Gudmundur. "Captured U-boats." U-boat.net. http://www.uboat.net/articles/index.html?article=32.

Hill, David. "Lighthouse Is Historically Notable." *Sun News*, Sunday, July 26, 1987.

Horry County Historical Society. *Independent Republic Quarterly.* Vols. 3, 4, 6, 9, 12, 14, 19 and 20 (1967 to present).

Horry Dispatch. May 9 1861.

Horry Herald. "Body Found on Strand." February 18, 1943.

———. "Give Wide Berth to Straying Bombs." June 25, 1942, 1.

———. "Rumors Float about Refuelling of Axis." July 25, 1942, 1.

Lennon, Gered. *Living with the South Carolina Coast.* Durham, NC: Duke University Press, 1996.

Linder, Suzanne, and Maria Thacker. *Historical Atlas of the Rice Plantations of Georgetown County and the Santee River.* Columbia: South Carolina Department of Archives and History, 2001.

Manigault Chapter of the United Daughters of the Confederacy. *For Love of a Rebel.* N.p., self-published, 1964.

McMillan, Susan. *Then and Now: Myrtle Beach and the Grand Strand.* Charleston, SC: Arcadia Publishing, 2007.

Mitchell, Mary, and Albert Goodrich. *The Remarkable Huntingtons: A Chronicle of Marriage.* Newport, RI: Budd Drive Press, 2004.

Moore, John Hammond. "Nazi Troopers in South Carolina." *South Carolina Historical Magazine* 81, no. 4 (October 1980): 306–15.

National Register of Historic Places Inventory–Nomination Form. "Battery White." South Carolina Department of Archives and History. http://www.nationalregister.sc.gov/georgetown/S10817722010/S10817722010.pdf.

Official Records of the Union and Confederate Navies in the War of the Rebellion. 30 vols. Washington, D.C.: U.S. Government Printing Office, 1894–1922.

Petit, James Percival, ed. *South Carolina and the Sea: Day by Day Toward Five Centuries, 1492–1985 A.D.* Vol. 2. Isle of Palms, SC: Le Petit Maison Publishers, Ltd., 1986.

Quattlebaum, Laura Janette. *The History of Horry County, South Carolina.* N.p., n.d.

Rhyne, Nancy. *The Grand Strand: An Uncommon Guide to Myrtle Beach and Its Surroundings*. Charlotte, NC: East Woods, 1981.

Rogers, George C., Jr. *The History of Georgetown County, South Carolina*. Columbia: University of South Carolina Press, 1970.

———. *Theodosia and Other Pee Dee Sketches*. Columbia, SC: R.L. Bryan Company, 1978.

Roske, Ralph J., and Charles Van Doren. *Lincoln's Commando: The Biography of Commander William B. Cushing USN*. New York: Harper and Row, 1957.

Salmon, Robin. E-mail message to author on Brookgreen Inquiry, September 21, 2009.

Shaum, Jack. E-mail messages to author on *The City of Richmond*, October 8, 2009, and January 23 and 25, 2010.

Simmons, Rick. "Did German U-Boats Patrol the Grand Strand During World War II?" *Alternatives* (July 9–26, 1987): 10–11, 20.

———. "Forgotten Island." *Alternatives* (September 2–16, 1988): 3, 17.

———. "The Hot and Hot Fish Club of All Saints." *Alternatives* (January 8–22, 1988): 3.

———. "Prince Frederick's Waccamaw Parish Church." *Alternatives* (August 7–21, 1987): 10–11.

———. "'Up Scope': Our Nazi U-Boat Scare." *Pee Dee* magazine (November–December 1992): 12–15.

Sloan, L.C. "Battery White, (1862–1865)." *Georgetown County Historic Register*, 1971.

South Carolina Department of Archives and History. "Battery White, Georgetown County." http://www.nationalregister.sc.gov/georgetown/S10817722010/index.htm.

Spence, Lee. *Shipwrecks, Pirates, & Privateers*. Charleston, SC: Narwhal Press, 1995.

Stokes, Barbara. *Myrtle Beach: A History, 1900–1980*. Columbia: University of South Carolina Press, 2007.

Tower, R. Lockwood. *A Carolinian Goes to War: The Civil War Narrative of Arthur Middleton Manigault*. Columbia: University of South Carolina Press, 1983.

The USS Harvest Moon. Harvest Moon Society. http://www.bjpeters.com/HarvestMoon.

The War of the Rebellion: A Compilation of the Official Records of the Union and Confederate Armies. 128 vols. Washington, D.C.: U.S. Government Printing Office, 1880–1901.

Wolf, Elizabeth Huntsinger. "Shipwrecks in Georgetown Waters." *Tidelands* magazine (2009): 18–21, 35–37.

About the Author

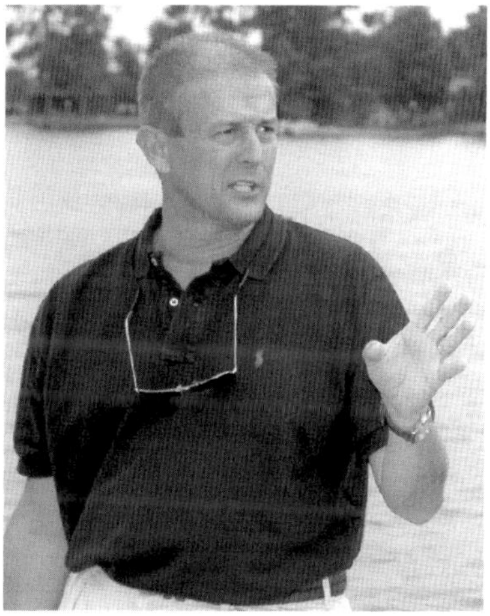

Dr. Rick Simmons was born and raised in South Carolina, and during the course of his education, he attended Clemson University, Coastal Carolina University and the University of South Carolina, where he completed his PhD in 1997. He lives in Louisiana with his wife, Sue, and his children, Courtenay and Cord, though he still spends a portion of the summer at his family home in Pawleys Island, South Carolina. He is the holder of the George K. Anding Endowed Professorship at Louisiana Tech University, where he is currently the director of the Honors Program as well as the director of the Center for Academic and Professional Development. This is his third book and second for The History Press; his first book for The History Press, *Defending South Carolina's Coast: The Civil War from Georgetown to Little River*, was published in 2009.